THE NEW BOOK OF
MEAT COOKERY

THE NEW BOOK OF
MEAT COOKERY

MARY BERRY

PUBLISHED IN ASSOCIATION WITH OXO

Queen Anne Press
Macdonald Futura Publishers
London

© Mary Berry/Brooke Bond Oxo Limited 1981

Edited by Kate Truman
Designed by Janet James

Cover photography by Paul Kemp. Back cover, top: Lemon
Chicken; bottom: Chinese Chicken (see page 178 for recipes).

ISBN 0362 00559 1

First published in 1981 by Queen Anne Press, Macdonald Futura
Publishers, Paulton House, 8 Shepherdess Walk, London N1 7LW

Typeset by Heavyweight Graphics
Colour by Cylinder
Printed and bound in Great Britain by Waterlow (Dunstable)
Limited

CONTENTS

ACKNOWLEDGEMENTS

The publishers would like to thank the following people and companies who were involved in the preparation of this book.

Photographer: Paul Kemp
Home economists: Rosemary Wadey and Elaine Bastable
Photographic stylist: Mary-Jane Kemp
Line drawings: Richard Jacobs
Wine writer: Anthony Hern of *The New Standard*

Kitchen equipment and accessories used in photography:
Divertimenti

There are a lot of recipes in this book, and each one has been tried and tested in my own kitchen. Without Clare Blunt, who helps me with the testing, the undertaking would have been impossible. My warmest thanks go to her for her hard work and unfailing good humour in every crisis. My thanks also go to both our families for their honest opinions on our efforts: to Clare's Kate and Timothy, and to my own Thomas, William and Annabel, sternest critics and staunchest fans.

Mary Berry

FOREWORD

Since Oxo first started to bring its special beefy goodness to your
meat cookery, much has changed in food and eating patterns, and
kitchen equipment has advanced considerably, too. In recent years
changes have occurred which even cookery experts would have
considered unlikely. Twenty years ago, for example, who'd have
thought that we would be eating Indian, Chinese, Italian, Greek
and American dishes at home, or that domestic kitchens would
contain freezers, food processors and other labour-saving devices?
But Oxo is as much at the heart of meat cookery today as it ever
was. That big beefy flavour gives a new dimension to your
cooking, whether you are making old favourites such as steak and
kidney pie or Lancashire hot pot, or a new dish like moussaka.

That's why Oxo is happy to be associated with *The New Book of
Meat Cookery.* From our close involvement with cooking trends
and our years of experience in the field of meat cookery, we hope
we can offer you as much help now as we've always done.
Whether you're a beginner or an accomplished cook, we're sure
you will find the step-by-step guides to basic and more complex
recipes useful and easy to follow. We know that Mary Berry, our
distinguished author, has tried to include all you need to know
about making your meat cookery easy, tasty and exciting.

INTRODUCTION

Nowadays, a wide variety of good quality meat is available in our shops. Never has it been so plentiful and easy to obtain, but never has it been so expensive. This is why it is important to understand what you are buying, to choose wisely and to know how to cook what you have bought. There is more to beef than rump steak and sirloin, and lamb is not limited to loin chops. There are expensive cuts of meat and cheaper ones; the latter are not inferior, they just need to be cooked differently. They should be cooked slowly for a long time on a bed of vegetables, with herbs and spices added to enhance the flavour. All this takes time - more time than a piece of tender fillet takes to grill - but the resulting gourmet dish is worth every extra minute.

The recipes contained in this book are ones that I have collected over the years: some are classic meat dishes, while there are others which I have developed myself. There are family favourites and special dishes for entertaining, and all meats, including poultry and game, are featured. My aim is to serve first-rate food: top quality ingredients cooked and presented as simply and perfectly as they can be. I'm not interested in over-elaborate recipes, since it is not my intention to spend all day in the kitchen. I prefer to have time to spare for my family and guests.

Neither do I want a kitchen full of cooking gadgets, half of which are never used, while the rest only add to the washing up. It has been said that all you need for good meat cookery is patience and a sharp knife, and I would suggest that, whatever tools you do buy, choose the best you can afford and they will repay you in full by lasting for years. One item of modern equipment that I most strongly recommend is a food processor. It will save you a great deal of time and effort in the preparation of food of all kinds. Chopping, mixing, blending and mincing are among the many operations which can be carried out in this simple and efficient machine.

However, the subject of this book is meat. Learn all you can about it by making a friend of your local butcher. Ask his advice and learn from what he has to say. The photographs and line drawings contained in this book will help you identify the various cuts of meat and the best ways to cook them. We have tried to present them as clearly and comprehensively as possible, and have included the newer cuts such as 'butterfly' lamb chops, and bacon chops. Study the sections on carving - it is a skill well worth learning. Good carving can make a joint go a long way and look appetising at the same time.

Above all, this book is for *you*; it is meant for your interest and your pleasure. Cookery to me is fun, and I'd like you to enjoy it, too.

Mary Berry

A GUIDE TO

BEEF

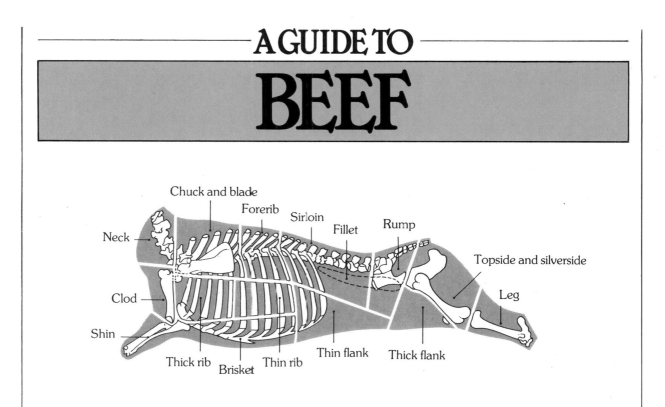

Neck · Chuck and blade · Forerib · Sirloin · Fillet · Rump · Topside and silverside · Leg · Clod · Shin · Thick rib · Brisket · Thin rib · Thin flank · Thick flank

BUYING

When you are buying beef – or lamb, pork, poultry, offal, veal or game for that matter – it pays to know what you are looking for. Do you want a prime joint for roasting, or something less expensive that will repay long, slow cooking? Do you know what good meat looks like in a shop?

Make a friend of your butcher and let him advise you. The good butcher is a craftsman and, if he knows you are interested, he will be glad to help. Don't be afraid to ask him questions; you can learn a lot from him, and a bit of expertise can only add interest to the routine shopping expedition.

To develop flavour and tenderness, some meat must be hung before it is sold; if cooked too soon after the animal has been slaughtered, the meat is tough and tasteless. The hanging period varies: beef is hung for a minimum of ten days, lamb for a minimum of four days and pork is not hung at all. It is, in fact, entirely the butcher's responsibility to ensure that the meat has been hung for the proper time. There are plenty of other things he can do for you, such as boning and rolling a joint for roasting, cutting steak into the size you want for a stew, mincing meats to individual requirements and, if you let him know in advance, he will prepare salt or pickled beef for boiling or a crown roast of lamb. Try to let him know your special requirements early in the week when the shop is less busy.

What to look for

The colour of beef is no guide to quality, as it varies from bright red to dark brown. When the meat is cut it develops a brownish-red colour when exposed to air, and for this reason some butchers use red tinted lights over the meat to enhance the redness. By law, no artificial colourings can be added to fresh meat to alter the colour.

The colour of the fat varies from one breed of animal to another. The fat of grass-fed beef is more yellow than that of barley-fed beef, which has a whiter fat and paler red meat. Some fat is essential to give the meat flavour. Recent research has revealed that there is no scientific foundation for the widely-held belief that a good flavour is only obtained from meat which is interspersed or marbled throughout with fat.

When buying beef, choose meat that has the amount of fat that your family prefers since it is obviously wasteful to buy a fatty joint if the fat is not going to be eaten. The most tender flesh is smooth and velvety, while cheaper cuts for slow cooking are coarser in texture. Pickled cuts are greyish in appearance and turn pinkish-red when cooked.

How much to buy

This depends very much on how you are going to serve the meat. If you are serving roast beef with a salad, you will need to buy more meat per person than if you are planning to serve it with roast

Rump steak

Sirloin steak (wi
– on the bo

Sirloin steaks – boned

Topside

Buy British Beef

Thin flank

Brisket – boned and rolled

's got the lot

Top rib

Back rib

Forerib – on the bone

Forerib – boned and rolled

Thick flank

Sirloin – boned and rolled

Sirloin – on the bone

Silverside

Skirt

Whole fillet

Blade (braising steaks)

Fillet steaks

Chuck steak

Clod

Leg

Mince

Neck

Shin

potatoes and a selection of vegetables. However, as a guide, allow 8-12 oz (225-350g) of beef on the bone per portion; 4-6 oz (100-150g) for boned and rolled beef; 6 oz (150g) for grilled steak; 6-8 oz (150-225g) for braised beef with the bone and 4-6 oz (100-150g) without the bone.

COOKING

Methods of cooking range from fast grilling or frying over fierce heat for tender steaks to long, slow cooking for the cheaper and tougher cuts.

Roasting

With beef, this falls into two categories: fast roasting, for the more expensive joints, and slow roasting (and pot roasting) for the less expensive, coarser joints. Meat cooked on the bone requires less cooking time than a boned and rolled joint because of the heat conduction from the bone.

Fast roasting
Roasting the prime cuts uncovered in a hot oven gives you crisp, brown meat on the outside, and you can decide how you want the meat in the centre to be done: rare and pinkish or well cooked throughout. Recent research has revealed that most people prefer the latter. The prime joints can be roasted satisfactorily at various oven temperatures because the texture of the meat is of such good quality, but it is sensible to roast in a hot oven if you are planning to serve Yorkshire pudding and roast potatoes with the meat since these must be cooked at a higher temperature. If a joint is cooked for a long time at a high temperature, there will be considerable shrinkage.

Preparation (fast roasting)
Season any fat on the meat with salt and freshly ground black pepper and place the joint on a rack

in a roasting tin. Roast in the oven, uncovered, according to the details below. Baste occasionally.

Roasting times (fast roasting)
These are for average roasts. If the joint is long and thin (such as the thin end of a rolled rib), cut the cooking time by about 5 minutes. If the joint is very thick (such as the thickest cut of rolled topside), increase the cooking time by about 5 minutes.

If you like really rare beef, cut the cooking time of the 'medium' details by 5 minutes per lb (450g).

To test that the beef is cooked
Pierce the thickest part of the joint with a fine skewer; if slightly pink-tinged juices run out, the meat is cooked and will be pink in the centre. If clear juices run out, the meat is cooked and will be well done throughout.

Suitable cuts (fast roasting): Sirloin, topside, fore rib, thick flank (the latter could be less tender than the others).

Slow roasting and pot roasting
It is better to cook the cheaper, coarser cuts in a cooler oven wrapped in foil or a roasting bag because the long, slow cooking tenderises the meat. The meat is first browned in hot fat on the hob or in the oven, then covered and cooked slowly in its own fat and steam - either in the oven or on the hob - to give a moist, tender joint. Unlike the fast roasting method, it is impossible to achieve meat that is well done, as the internal temperature reached would be insufficient to cook the meat this much.

Preparation (slow roasting)
Season any fat on the meat with salt and freshly ground black pepper. Melt some dripping or lard in

Roasting times (fast roasting)

Approximate weight of beef joint	Oven temperature	Approximate cooking time	
		Medium	Well done
1 lb (450g)	400°F (200°C) mark 6	45 minutes	1 hour 10 minutes
2 lb (900g)	400°F (200°C) mark 6	1 hour 15 minutes	1 hour 40 minutes
3 lb (1.4kg)	400°F (200°C) mark 6	1 hour 30 minutes	2 hours
4 lb (1.8kg)	400°F (200°C) mark 6	1 hour 45 minutes	2 hours 20 minutes
Over 4 lb (1.8kg)	400°F (200°C) mark 6	13 minutes per lb (450g)	18 minutes per lb (450g)

Roasting times (slow roasting)

Approximate weight of beef joint	Oven temperature	Approximate cooking time
1 lb (450g)	325°F (160°C) mark 3	2 hours
2 lb (900g)	325°F (160°C) mark 3	2 hours 30 minutes
3 lb (1.4kg)	325°F (160°C) mark 3	3 hours
4 lb (1.8kg)	325°F (160°C) mark 3	4 hours
Over 4 lb (1.8kg)	325°F (160°C) mark 3	1 hour per lb (450g)

a thick-bottomed pan on the hob or in a roasting tin or casserole in a hot oven (425°F [220°C] mark 7). Add the meat, turning it to brown on all sides, then cover with a lid or foil and cook gently on the hob or roast according to the details above.

Roasting times (slow roasting)
These are for average roasts. If the joint is long and thin, cut the cooking time by about 5 minutes. If the joint is very thick, increase the cooking time by about 5 minutes.

To test that the beef is cooked
Pierce the thickest part of the joint with a fine skewer; if clear juices run out, the meat is cooked. If the juices are slightly pink-tinged, continue cooking until they are clear.

Suitable cuts (slow roasting): Silverside, thick flank, thick rib, thin rib, brisket.

Grilling

This is a good method of cooking the tender and juicy cuts. It involves cooking quickly (8–15 minutes, according to taste and thickness) by radiant heat – nowadays usually under a fixed electric or gas grill – although the original method of cooking over glowing charcoal, as in a barbecue, gives a special flavour. Very lean meat should be brushed first with oil. Turn once during cooking.

Suitable cuts: Fillet steak, rump steak, sirloin steak.

Frying

Again, this is a good method of cooking the tender and juicy cuts. It is best to use a really heavy pan or ribbed metal griddle, which should first be heated, then rubbed with a small amount of butter or oil. Fry, turning once, until the meat is done to your liking.

Suitable cuts: Fillet steak, rump steak, sirloin steak.

Braising

This is a slow, gentle method of cooking the tougher and less expensive cuts of meat. It involves a combination of baking and steaming in a small amount of liquid, with the addition of herbs, vegetables and seasonings which blend together during the cooking time to give flavour and succulence to the meat. Use a heavy casserole with a tight-fitting lid if you are cooking in the oven or a heavy, thick-bottomed saucepan if you are using the hob.

Trim any excess fat from the meat. Melt a little oil or fat in the casserole or saucepan, add the meat and fry to brown. Fry peeled and sliced or diced vegetables such as onions, carrots, turnips and parsnips in the oil or fat. Drain off the fat and place the meat on top of the vegetables. Add stock, beer, cider or wine to cover the vegetables and season with salt, freshly ground black pepper and herbs. Cover with the tight-fitting lid and cook very slowly in the oven at 325°F (160°C) mark 3 or cook gently on the hob.

Suitable cuts: Thick rib, topside, silverside, chuck and blade, flank, brisket.

Stews and casseroles

These require long, slow cooking and are most suitable for the toughest and least expensive cuts. The meat is cooked in liquid, with vegetables, flavourings, herbs and spices, and sometimes flour or another thickening agent is added. Stews are simmered on the hob for a long time: sometimes for longer than four hours. This is the method used for curries, ragouts, goulashes and hot pots, and the keys to success are well-flavoured stock or liquid, and very slow cooking.

Casseroles are cooked slowly in the oven using a thick, strong dish covered by a tight-fitting lid. It should be remembered that a casserole cooked in a deep dish will take longer to cook than one cooked in a shallow dish.

Suitable cuts: Leg, flank, chuck and blade, skirt, shin.

Boiling

Boiling meat involves simmering it on very low heat. This method is used for tougher, whole joints. Water is poured into the pan to just cover the meat, is then brought to the boil, vegetables such as whole carrots, onions stuck with cloves, parsley and bayleaf are added and the meat is then simmered for 40 minutes per lb (450g) plus an extra 40 minutes for small joints. Other vegetables may be added for the last hour of the cooking time. The meat is served with the vegetables and some of the cooking liquor thickened to make a sauce.

This method is particularly suitable for cooking joints such as salted silverside and brisket. Sometimes topside is boiled although it is more usually roasted. If your butcher tells you that the joint is somewhat salty, bring the meat and water to the boil, discard the water, add fresh, cold water and continue as above.

Suitable cuts: Silverside, brisket (both salted), tongue.

Minced beef

Butchers often sell two grades of minced beef, the higher quality usually being known as 'best' or 'lean' mince. It is generally leaner and is darker red than the other quality which contains more fat and some connective tissue. If you buy a pack labelled merely 'mince,' it will usually contain a mixture of beef, lamb, pork and perhaps heart or other offal. It can be very tasty when used as a base for stuffing vegetables such as marrow or peppers, and is also the cheapest to buy. You may prefer to buy the meat in one piece and either have your butcher mince it for you, or to mince it at home yourself in a food processor or mincer. Mince does not keep well out of the freezer, so you should use it on the same day it is bought or minced at home. If you are mincing cooked meat, chill it first to make it firm. Mince in a food processor or mincer, including the amount of fat you like, then blend with a sauce. Season with salt and freshly ground black pepper and use as a filling for pasties and pies.

CARVING

Good carving is a skill which can be acquired quite easily with practice, a really sharp knife and an effective knife sharpener. The blade of the knife should be slightly flexible, and made of best stainless or carbon steel. It should be well-balanced and feel comfortable in the hand. Matching carving sets are not important: the essentials are a sharp-bladed knife, a safe fork with a guard and a good sharpener (see page 48). If possible, sharpen the knife while the joint is cooking so there is not a rush to get everything done when the joint is waiting to be carved.

Finally, you need confidence, which comes from practice and a knowledge of the anatomy of the joint you are carving. If, for example, you are carving a leg, think of the animal and you will know where to expect the bone to be. Carving a hot joint must be done quickly if everyone is to have their fair share while it is still hot, and the slices should look good, too. Where possible, cut the meat across the grain to shorten the fibres and make the meat seem more tender. Boned and rolled joints are obviously easier to carve than meat on the bone. But the aim in both cases should be to cut good sized, uniform slices – try to avoid untidy little bits – of the correct thickness. Beef should be carved in moderately thick slices. After cooking, cover the joint with foil or a large heatproof dish or basin, keep warm in the oven and allow it to 'rest' for about 10 minutes before carving.

LEFT-OVERS

This is where the cook has a chance to show her ingenuity. There is endless scope for making appetising dishes using left-over meat, and it is particularly satisfying to know that nothing has been wasted. Take the trouble to present left-over dishes attractively, using colourful garnishes such as slices of red and green pepper, chopped tomatoes or gherkins. Small triangles of toast or croûtons of fried bread enhance the appearance of hot mince dishes. Casseroles, curries and stews are often better when served on the second day. Care should be taken to reheat them thoroughly in a hot oven until the liquid has boiled for at least 10 minutes.

Cold beef - roasted or boiled, salt or fresh - is a perfect accompaniment for any salad. Slice it and serve with pickles, chutney or horseradish sauce. Slices of rare or salt beef can be served with potato salad and they make delicious sandwiches with pickles, horseradish sauce or mustard. Or you could mince odd pieces, mix them with chutney and use as a sandwich topping. Chopped or cubed beef makes a ragout or hash; cooked mince provides the foundation for a vast number of recipes, including cottage pie, or delicious terrines and pâtés.

The general principles of carving are very simple, and can be applied to most joints of meat.

1 After cooking, allow the joint to 'rest' for about 10 minutes before carving to make the meat firmer and easier to carve.

2 After cooking, remove any string. Remove the chine bone which will have been chopped through by the butcher.

3 Carve on a flat, slip-proof surface such as a wooden board, using a sharp knife and a fork with a safety guard.

4 Run a sharp knife between the meat and bones to loosen the meat, loosening only as much meat as you're likely to need for one meal.

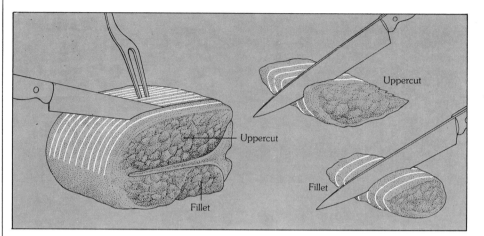

SIRLOIN

Usually bought boned and rolled, in which case simply carve in slices. If bought on the bone, remove any string, run the knife down either side of the bone to loosen the meat and carve in slices (left). Alternatively, run the knife down either side of the bone, lift off the meat and carve in slices (right).

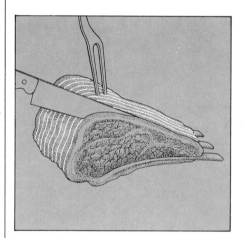

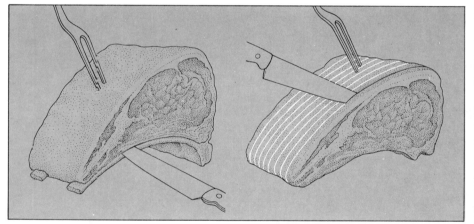

WING RIB

Remove the chine bone which will have been chopped through by the butcher. Run the knife between the meat and ribs to loosen the meat. Don't loosen more than you're likely to need for one meal. Carve in slices.

FORERIB

Remove the chine bone which will have been chopped through by the butcher. Run the knife between the meat and bones to free the meat (left). Don't loosen more than you're likely to need for one meal. Carve in slices (right).

A GUIDE TO
LAMB

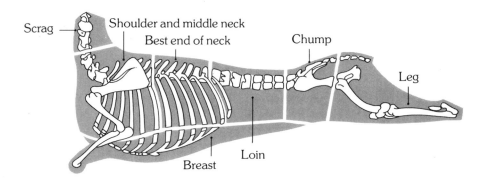

Scrag — Shoulder and middle neck — Best end of neck — Chump — Leg — Loin — Breast

BUYING

Good quality lamb is easy to find. It is consistently tender and well-flavoured whether you buy the home-bred variety from England, Scotland or Wales which is available in the shops in spring, summer and autumn, or the excellent imported lamb from New Zealand, available from January to May.

Mutton, once a traditional dish in Britain, is difficult to obtain nowadays. There is so little demand for it that many butchers are reluctant to stock it. It has, however, a distinctive flavour that many people enjoy.

What to look for

The flesh of a very young lamb is light pink, the fat is creamy white and there is a blue tinge in the knuckle bones in legs and shoulders. In an older animal the flesh is darker, varying from light to dark red, depending on the breed of sheep and how it has been fed. Legs and shoulders should be plump, and a layer of fat should cover the meat.

Mutton joints are larger, the flesh is darker and coarser in texture, and there is a large proportion of fat distributed throughout the meat. It must be well hung. Leg of mutton is usually pot roasted or boiled.

How much to buy

As a guide, allow about 8 oz (255g) per portion for leg and shoulder roasts; 5 oz (125g) for boned roasts; 5 oz (125g) for boneless meats for stews and casseroles and 7 oz (200g) with the bone; 4–5 oz (100–125g) for minced lamb; 2 loin chops per person.

COOKING

Roasting

Leg of lamb is a traditional roast, as the meat is tender and well-flavoured, but shoulder, best end of neck and loin are every bit as tasty and are even easier to carve if they are boned and rolled. Any cut of lamb - except scrag and middle neck - is suitable for roasting and no extra fat should be needed. Some people like lamb to be slightly underdone, but most seem to prefer it well done throughout.

Preparation

Season with salt and freshly ground black pepper and sprinkle with a little dried rosemary, if liked. Place the joint on a rack in a roasting tin, and roast, uncovered, according to the details (right). Baste occasionally.

Roasting times

Approximate weight of lamb joint	Oven temperature	Approximate cooking time
1 lb (450g)	350°F (180°C) mark 4	1 hour
2 lb (900g)	350°F (180°C) mark 4	1 hour 20 minutes
3 lb (1.4kg)	350°F (180°C) mark 4	1 hour 40 minutes
4 lb (1.8kg)	350°F (180°C) mark 4	2 hours 30 minutes
Over 4 lb (1.8kg)	350°F (180°C) mark 4	25 minutes per lb (450g)

Roasting times
These are for average roasts. If the joint is long and thin, cut the cooking time by about 5 minutes. If the joint is very thick, increase the cooking time by about 5 minutes.

To test that the lamb is cooked
Pierce the thickest part of the joint with a fine skewer; if clear juices run out, the meat is cooked. If the juices are slightly pink-tinged, continue cooking until they are clear, unless you like lamb underdone.

Suitable cuts: All lamb cuts except scrag and middle neck.

Grilling and frying

A fierce heat is needed and the cooking time should be short. To check that the lamb is cooked, pierce with a fine skewer; if clear juices run out, the meat is cooked. If the juices are slightly pink-tinged, continue cooking until they are clear.

Loin chops are recognisable by the short T-shaped bone and eye of lean on either side of it. Chump chops, which come from the top of the leg, are very lean, oval in shape, and have a small round bone. Best end of neck cutlets are recognisable by a round 'eye' with a tiny dot of lean beneath and a long rib bone, and are used for preparing a guard of honour, a crown roast and noisettes.

Suitable cuts: Chops (loin or chump), best end of neck cutlets, boneless slices from the top of the leg, shoulder, leg (the latter two for kebabs).

Braising

Any cut of lamb is suitable for this method, whether boned and rolled or on the bone. Remember to remove all the excess fat first before cooking, otherwise the meat may be greasy.

Pot roasting

This is a very similar method to braising and again a strong, thick-bottomed pan will be needed. Remove all the fat from the meat. Melt a little oil or fat in the pan and fry the meat until brown. Cover with a tight-fitting lid and cook on low heat. Herbs, whole vegetables and seasonings can be added to taste, and the meat will cook gently in its own steam.

Suitable cuts: Any cuts except scrag and middle neck are suitable for this method.

Stews and casseroles

Cooking lamb by either of these methods should be slow, but not as slow as for beef (see page 13). A good lamb stew can be cooked in 1½-2 hours. Goulashes, hot pots and curries are included in this classification, as these strongly-flavoured dishes improve with long cooking allowing the spices to penetrate the meat. Remember to remove all excess fat.

Suitable cuts: Breast, scrag, middle neck.

Boiling

This method is used for mutton and involves simmering the meat over very low heat. See the method given for beef (page 14).

Suitable cuts: Leg of mutton.

Pies

Use leg or shoulder of lamb with most of the fat removed.

British Lamb mint condition

Breast – on the bone

Leg

Breast – boned, rolled and stuffed

Crown roast

Scrag end of neck

Middle neck chops

Chump chops

Best end of neck cutlets

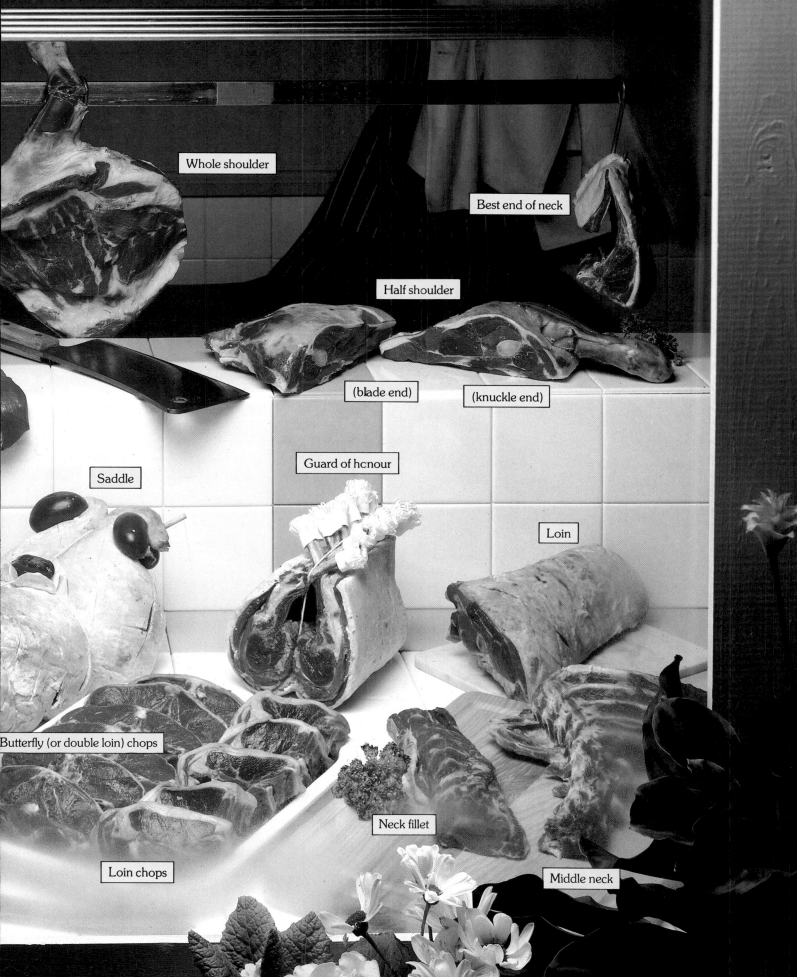

Whole shoulder

Best end of neck

Half shoulder

(blade end)

(knuckle end)

Guard of hcnour

Saddle

Loin

Butterfly (or double loin) chops

Neck fillet

Loin chops

Middle neck

CARVING

Aim at cutting slices of lamb about ¼ in. (0.6cm) thick. With a loin or best end of neck joint, ask your butcher to chine the bone first. Chining means partly chopping through the backbone lengthwise so the bone can be removed before carving to make the meat easier to slice between the ribs. Carving a shoulder which contains the bone is more difficult; if you doubt your ability, ask your butcher to bone and roll the joint for you. After cooking, cover the joint with foil or a large heatproof dish or basin; keep warm in the oven and allow it to 'rest' for about 10 minutes before carving.

LEFT-OVERS

Cold roast lamb may be sliced and served with salads and pickles, or the meat may be minced and used to make shepherd's pie. Any meat left from a lamb casserole makes a good shepherd's pie, too, or it can be used to stuff courgettes or aubergines. Minced left-over lamb is suitable for making all kinds of pies and pâtés, while curries, stews, ragouts and hot pots reheat satisfactorily.

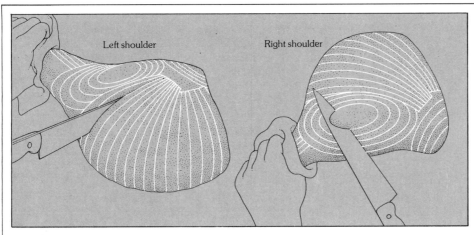

Left shoulder Right shoulder

SHOULDER
Before cooking, cut round the blade bone to loosen the meat, but leave the bone in place. After cooking, twist and pull out the blade to make carving simpler. Turn the joint so the skin side is uppermost and firmly hold the shank end with a carving fork or, if preferred, in a cloth. Carve a wedge-shaped slice (about ¼ in. [0.6cm] thick) from the centre, then continue carving slices from either side of this cut. Carve horizontal slices from the shank end, then small, vertical slices from beside the bone. Turn the joint over, remove any fat, then carve in horizontal slices.

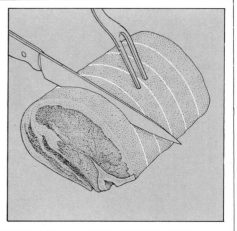

BEST END OF NECK AND LOIN
Remove the chine bone which will have been loosened by the butcher, then carve between the ribs to divide the joint into cutlets.

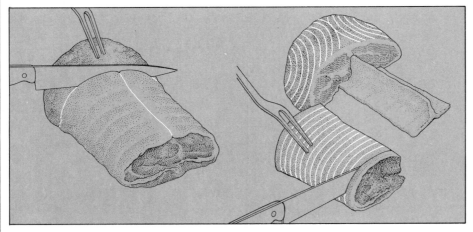

SADDLE
Cut across the base down to the bone, then make a cut along the backbone (left). Run the knife between meat and bone, lift off the meat and carve in slices. Leave the base of the saddle on the bone and carve horizontal slices from it (right).

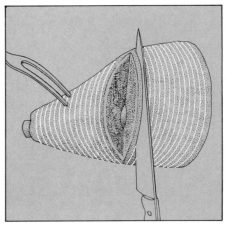

LEG
Firmly hold the knuckle end with a carving fork or, if preferred, in a cloth. Carve a wedge-shaped slice (about ¼ in. [0.6cm] thick) from the centre of the meatiest side, then continue carving slices from either side of this cut. Turn the joint over, remove any fat, then carve in horizontal slices.

A GUIDE TO

PORK

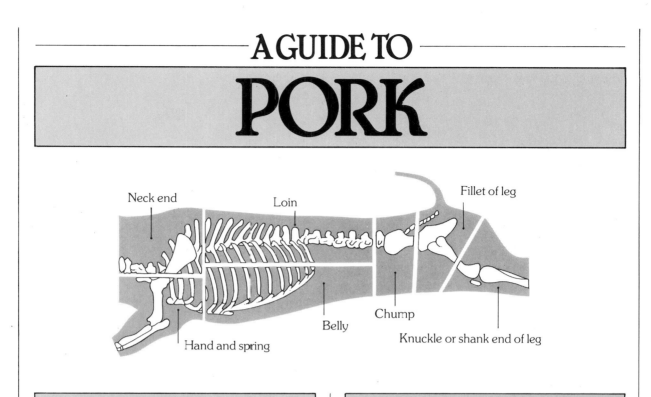

Neck end · Loin · Fillet of leg · Hand and spring · Belly · Chump · Knuckle or shank end of leg

BUYING

Almost all of the pig – from the head to the trotters – can be eaten, either as fresh pork or cured as bacon and ham. With today's efficient refrigeration, pork can be transported and stored safely and is consequently available throughout the year. It gives very good value for money in the summer.

What to look for

The lean meat should be pale pink, smooth and finely grained, and the fat should be white and firm. Choose meat which is not too fatty. Pork joints may be boned and rolled, but those cooked on the bone have the best flavour.

How much to buy

As a guide, allow 8-12 oz (225-350g) per portion for pork on the bone and 4-6 oz (100-175g) without the bone.

COOKING

Roasting

Ask your butcher to score the rind evenly and deeply, then follow the instructions below for really crisp crackling.

Preparation

Brush the skin with oil and sprinkle with salt. Lift off the skin with a sharp knife, then replace on the meat before roasting. Place the joint on a rack in a roasting tin and roast in the oven according to the details below. Do not baste during cooking. When the joint is cooked, the crackling can be easily snipped with scissors or a sharp knife.

Roasting times

These are for average roasts. If the joint is long and thin, cut the cooking time by about 5 minutes. If the joint is very thick, increase the cooking time by about 5 minutes.

Roasting times

Approximate weight of pork joint	Oven temperature	Approximate cooking time
1 lb (450g)	350°F (180°C) mark 4	1 hour 10 minutes
2 lb (900g)	350°F (180°C) mark 4	1 hour 30 minutes
3 lb (1.4kg)	350°F (180°C) mark 4	2 hours
4 lb (1.8kg)	350°F (180°C) mark 4	2 hours 40 minutes
Over 4 lb (1.8kg)	350°F (180°C) mark 4	30 minutes per lb (450g)

Leg – on the bone

Loin – boned and rolled

Spare ribs (Chinese style)

Slices of belly – boned

Leg (fillet end) – boned and rolled

Belly – boned, rolled and stuffed

Whole leg – boned and rolled

Fillet (or tenderloin)

Spare rib – boned and rolled

Loin – on the bone

British Pork

Hand and spring

Belly – on the bone

Blade

Spare rib chops (British style)

Chump chops

Loin chops

To test that the pork is cooked

Pierce the thickest part of the joint with a fine skewer; if clear juices run out, the meat is cooked. If the juices are slightly pink-tinged, continue cooking until they are clear as pork should *never* be undercooked.

Suitable cuts: Leg, loin, spare rib and blade bone, hand and spring.

Grilling

Grill slowly under a moderate grill for about 15-20 minutes, so that the meat in the centre is thoroughly cooked by the time the outside is well browned.

Suitable cuts: Loin chops, chump chops, leg steaks, slices of belly, spare rib chops.

Frying

Trim off the skin and any excess fat and place these pieces in a frying pan. Cook until the fat has run out. If preferred use enough melted fat or oil to barely cover the bottom of the pan. Quickly brown the meat, reduce the heat and continue cooking, turning once. The pan may be covered with a lid.

Suitable cuts: Loin and chump chops, fillet, leg steaks, thin slices of belly.

Braising and pot roasting

See the methods given for beef (pages 12 and 13).

Suitable cuts: Small, whole joints such as hand and spring, spare rib, other boned and rolled joints.

Stews and casseroles

See the methods given for beef (page 13).

Suitable cuts: Hand and spring, belly, shoulder (all with fat removed).

Boiling

See the method given for beef (page 14). Boil for 25-30 minutes per lb (450g) plus an extra 30 minutes.

Suitable cuts: Salt pork joints.

Pies and patties

Mince any lean pork for use in pies and patties.

CARVING

After cooking, cover the joint with foil or a large heatproof dish or basin, keep warm in the oven and allow it to 'rest' for about 10 minutes before carving.

LEFT-OVERS

Cold pork is very good with salads of all kinds.

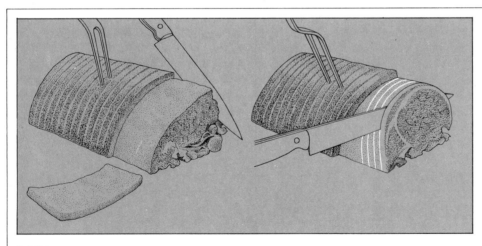

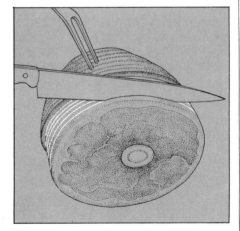

LOIN
Remove the chine bone. Remove the crackling in sections. Don't remove more than you're likely to need for one meal. Run the knife between meat and bones (left) to free the meat, then carve in slices (right). Give each person some crackling.

LEG
Remove the crackling in sections. Don't remove more than you're likely to need for one meal. Carve from the widest end of the joint, where the neatly severed bone can be seen. When the knuckle end of the bone is reached, carve down to and slightly around the bone. Turn the joint over and repeat, aiming to keep the cut end of the joint level above and below the knuckle bone. At the knuckle end, carve slices slanting towards the neatly severed bone.

A GUIDE TO

BACON

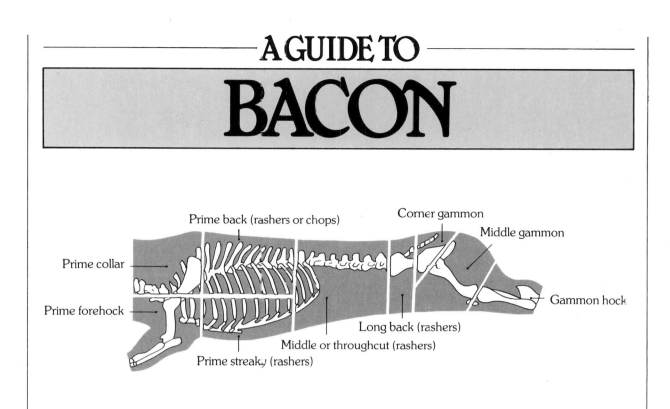

Prime back (rashers or chops)
Corner gammon
Middle gammon
Prime collar
Prime forehock
Gammon hock
Long back (rashers)
Middle or throughcut (rashers)
Prime streaky (rashers)

BUYING

Bacon is the flesh of a pig which has been salted or cured in brine and then smoked. Green bacon is cured but not smoked. Gammon is the hind leg which is cured on the side of bacon and, when cooked and served cold, the gammon becomes known as ham. For special hams, such as the York and Bradenham varieties, the leg of the pig is cooked and cured separately to individual manufacturers' special recipes. Shoulder and collar are less expensive cuts prepared in the same way and are particularly good for boiling.

What to look for

The lean meat, fat and rind should all be firm. The fat should be white and the rind thin. The rind of green bacon is white and the lean dark pink. Smoked bacon has golden brown rind and brownish pink lean which sometimes has a lustre as a result of the smoking. Most bacon joints are already boned when you buy them.

SOAKING

Ask your butcher whether he recommends you to soak the piece of bacon that you buy. Usually a large gammon should be soaked in cold water for 24 hours, whereas a smaller joint will only have to be soaked overnight or for 12 hours. Sweetcure or mildcure joints do not have to be soaked at all. For vacuum-packed bacon, follow the instructions on the pack for soaking.

If you think your bacon joint is salty and you cannot spare the time to soak it, use this quick method for getting rid of some of the salt. Place the joint in a pan of cold water and bring slowly to the boil, then drain off all the water. Cover the joint with fresh, cold water, bring to the boil, reduce the heat and simmer according to the details overleaf.

COOKING

Grilling

For gammon, use rashers ¼-½ in. (0.6-1.25cm) thick. Soak in cold water for 1 hour if they are salty. Turn them frequently during cooking, which should take about 15–20 minutes, according to thickness.

For bacon, remove the rind and any pieces of bone and discard. Overlap the rashers in the grill pan and turn once during cooking.

Suitable cuts: Gammon steaks, prime streaky, prime back, long back, middle cut.

Frying

Remove the rind and any pieces of bone and discard. Heat enough oil or fat to barely cover the bottom of a frying pan. Overlap the rashers in the

Whole gammon (smoked)

Pork chipolatas

Gammon hock (smoked)

Slipper (smoked)

Whole prime forehock (smoked)

Prime forehock (green), cut in half

Middle (or through) cut rashers

Streaky rashers (green)

Prime back rashers (green)

Prime back rashers (smoked)

Streaky rashers (smoked)

Beef sausages

Pork sausages

Prime collar (smoked)

Middle gammon (smoked)

Hocks (green)

Hocks (smoked)

Gammon steaks

Bacon chops

Gammon rashers

Long back rashers

pan and turn once during cooking.

Suitable cuts: Gammon steaks, prime streaky, prime back, long back, middle cut.

Boiling

For gammon, soak the joint in cold water for 24 hours. Place in a saucepan of fresh, cold water and bring to the boil. Reduce the heat and simmer very gently for about 2½ hours for a whole gammon, or for about 20 minutes per lb (450g) plus an extra 20 minutes for smaller joints. Remove from the heat and leave in the pan for 1 hour. Remove the rind, sprinkle with brown sugar, stick with cloves and brown in a hot oven for 20 minutes or until golden brown. Alternatively, use the old-fashioned haybox method (*see recipe on page 150*) which prevents shrinkage and gives excellent results.

Suitable cuts: Middle gammon, corner gammon, gammon hock, slipper, prime collar.

CARVING

Ham should be carved in very thin slices, using a special ham knife if possible.

LEFT-OVERS

Sliced, chopped or minced ham makes excellent sandwich fillings, especially if pickles, gherkins, chutney, mustard sauce, apple or pineapple are added. Use chopped ham or bacon in risottos and omelettes. Serve cold ham with salads of all kinds.

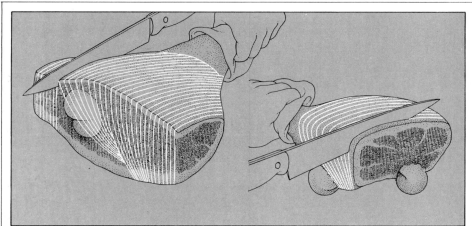

PRIME FOREHOCK
Carve with the fat side underneath. Firmly hold the protruding bone with a carving fork or, if preferred, in a cloth. Carve in vertical slices up to the bone, then repeat from the other end. When the bone is reached, carve long, downward-slanting slices at an angle to the bone. Turn the joint over and carve in slices down to the bone.

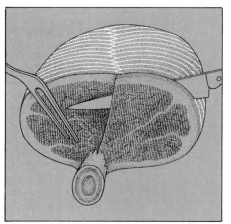

WHOLE GAMMON
If already boned, simply carve in thin slices. If bought on the bone, remove a small slice from the knuckle end of the bone. Carve in long, oblique slices down to the bone on either side of it.

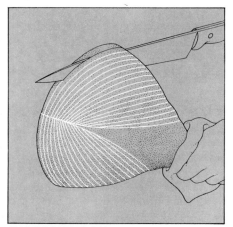

GAMMON HOCK
Firmly hold the shank end with a fork or, if preferred, in a cloth. Carve in wedge-shaped slices from one side of the bone. Turn the joint over and repeat.

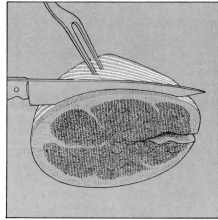

CORNER GAMMON
Carve in wedge-shaped slices which are thicker on the wider curve and thinner on the side from which the bone has been removed.

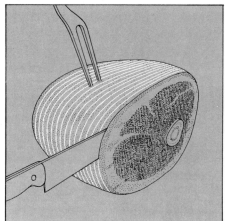

MIDDLE GAMMON
Carve in slices down to and around the bone.

POULTRY

Chicken, turkey and duck are on our tables at all times of the year, and goose is a Christmas treat. Modern methods of rearing and refrigeration mean that poultry is available throughout the country and is of uniform quality. It is one of the most valuable foods we have: it contains more protein per ounce than beef, eggs, cheese or milk.

Poultry is extremely versatile in cooking and its tender flesh takes kindly to all manner of flavourings. The bland meat of chicken and turkey forms a background for spicy flavourings, herb stuffings and rich sauces, while the rather fatty flesh of duck and goose calls for the refreshing contrast of fruit –apple, orange or cranberry sauce, orange salad, cherries or prune stuffing. When you are roasting a bird, remember that chicken and turkey flesh is lean and dry and needs the protection of cooking foil or a coat of bacon rashers, while the fatty flesh of duck or goose needs neither.

STUFFING

Roast poultry benefits from a good stuffing for several reasons. It helps to maintain the shape of the bird, keeps it moist during cooking, adds flavour and interest and increases the number of portions. Stuff the neck cavity only as it then cooks more quickly and is easier to carve.

Chicken

The chickens sold today are nearly always young birds, with a delicate flavour. The flesh is tender and should never be overcooked. You can buy them as whole birds or as chicken pieces, and they may be either fresh or frozen. Buying a whole bird is more economical if you are catering for a family, as it will provide more than one meal. Chicken pieces, which can be grilled or fried, are a good choice for a quick meal.

As the name implies, oven-ready, frozen chickens are sold ready-cleaned, usually with the giblets packed separately. Fresh chickens may be ready-trussed before you buy them, or your butcher may prepare and truss the bird for you in the shop.

Make sure that the giblets are included as they are useful when making the gravy. Fresh chickens have a succulent flavour but are considerably more expensive. Frozen birds, if cooked with care and served with a well-flavoured stuffing or a spicy sauce, can be excellent. A fresh chicken will keep for up to two days in the refrigerator but remember that *a frozen bird must be completely thawed before cooking*. Leave it in its wrappings and, for a 2 lb (900g) bird, allow to thaw for about nine hours in a warm kitchen or for 24 hours in the refrigerator. Chicken joints take about three or four hours to thaw.

How much to buy

Birds are usually chosen by weight. As a guide, allow about 8 oz (225g) of oven-ready chicken per portion. A 2½-3 lb (1.1-1.4kg) oven-ready chicken will provide one meal for four people; a 4 lb (1.8kg) bird will provide up to two meals per person.

Poussin: This is a young bird up to six weeks old, weighing up to 1½ lb (675g). They are very tender and are particularly suitable for grilling. Allow one small bird per person, or split a bigger bird down the centre and give a leg and wing to each person.

Capon: This is a cock bird especially reared to produce more meat to the bone. It is economical for a larger family roast.

Boiling fowl: This is a retired breeding bird aged over 12 months and weighing 5-6 lb (2.3-2.7kg). A boiling fowl must be cooked slowly for a long time, so is best used in casseroles. It has a good flavour.

Boiling hen: This is a former egg-laying bird which is smaller than a boiling fowl. It is also suitable for boiling or stewing.

COOKING

Chicken can be roasted, grilled, casseroled or boiled. It may be used in innumerable made-up dishes such as stuffed peppers and savoury pancakes, so left-overs are never a problem. It is delicious cold.

Boiling fowl

Duck

Turkey

Capon

Chicken

Chicken leg

Poussin

Chicken thigh

Goose

Chicken wing

Chicken breast – boneless

Chicken drumstick

Roasting times

Approximate weight of chicken	Oven temperature	Approximate cooking time
2½ lb (1.1kg)	400°F (200°C) mark 6	55 minutes
3½ lb (1.6kg)	400°F (200°C) mark 6	1 hour 15 minutes
4 lb (1.8kg)	400°F (200°C) mark 6	1 hour 35 minutes
5 lb (2.3kg)	400°F (200°C) mark 6	2 hours
6 lb (2.7kg)	400°F (200°C) mark 6	2 hours 15 minutes
Over 6 lb (2.7kg)	375°F (190°C) mark 5	20 minutes per lb (450g)

Roasting

Preparation

Remember to *completely thaw a frozen chicken before roasting*. If you are using stuffing, weigh the bird after you have stuffed it and use this weight to calculate the roasting time. Truss with small skewers or string and lightly spread the breast with butter or bacon fat. Season with salt and freshly ground black pepper and roast, basting occasionally, according to the details above. If the breast and thighs appear to be getting too brown, cover with foil.

To test that the chicken is cooked

Pierce the thickest part of the thigh with a fine skewer; if clear juices run out, the chicken is cooked. If the juices are slightly pink-tinged, continue cooking until they are clear. After cooking, cover the chicken with foil, keep warm in the oven and allow it to 'rest' for about 10 minutes before carving (see page 33).

Turkey

Turkey used to be regarded as a seasonal bird, confined to the traditional Christmas dinner. Nowadays, however, turkey can be found in the shops throughout the year. Although fresh turkeys are still most plentiful around Christmas, breeders are also producing relatively small birds with a good plump breast, which are available frozen and oven-ready all through the year. These are particularly economical if you are entertaining a number of people. In addition, frozen roasts of boned and rolled turkey meat are available. These are easy to cook, carve and serve and there is no waste. Some good supermarkets also stock turkey portions of sliced breast or drumsticks, which are excellent in casseroles and curries.

If you are buying a fresh turkey, order it well in advance from your butcher or poulterer and ask him to draw it for you. Check that it has a plump breast of white, unblemished skin. Fresh turkey will keep for up to three days in the refrigerator, but remember that *a frozen turkey must be completely thawed before cooking*. Leave it in its wrappings and allow plenty of time for thawing. You should allow a large bird over 12 lb (4.7kg) in weight to thaw for three days, and a smaller bird up to 12 lb (4.7kg) will need 30 hours in which to thaw.

How much to buy

As a guide, a 6-8 lb (2.7-3.5kg) oven-ready turkey will give 8-12 servings; a 10-13 lb (4.5-5.9kg) oven-ready bird will give 15-20 servings; a 14-20 lb (6.5-9kg) oven-ready bird will give 20-30 servings.

COOKING

Turkey can be roasted, grilled, casseroled or boiled.

Roasting

Preparation

Remember to completely thaw a frozen turkey before cooking. If you are using stuffing, weigh the bird after you have stuffed it and use this weight to calculate the roasting time. Truss with small skewers or string and place on a rack in a roasting tin. Brush the skin with melted butter and season with salt and freshly ground black pepper. Cover loosely with foil, place in the oven on a shelf just below the middle and roast according to the details overleaf. Open the foil for the last 1¼ hours of cooking time for a larger bird (over 10 lb [4.5kg] in weight) and for the last 50 minutes for a smaller bird. Baste occasionally.

Roasting times

Approximate weight of turkey	Oven temperature	Approximate cooking time
5 lb (2.3kg)	350°F (180°C) mark 4	2 hours 30 minutes
10 lb (4.5kg)	350°F (180°C) mark 4	3 hours 15 minutes
15 lb (6.8kg)	350°F (180°C) mark 4	4 hours
20 lb (9kg)	325°F (160°C) mark 3	5 hours

To test that the turkey is cooked
Pierce the thickest part of the thigh with a fine skewer; if clear juices run out, the turkey is cooked. If the juices are slightly pink-tinged, continue cooking until they are clear. After cooking, cover the turkey with foil, keep warm in the oven and allow it to 'rest' for 10 minutes before carving (see facing page).

——————— Duck ———————

Duck is now available throughout the year, since young tender birds are reared especially for freezing. The flesh is dark and fatty compared with that of chicken, and there is less meat on the bird but the flavour is excellent.

How much to buy

A 4-5 lb (1.8-2.3kg) oven-ready, frozen duck will serve four people. Try roasting it with pork to feed more people. Buy a 1½-2 lb (675-900g) piece of boned belly of pork or a 1½-2 lb (675-900g) piece of boned and rolled spare rib. Roast side by side in a roasting tin for 45 minutes at 400°F (200°C) mark 6. Reduce the oven temperature to 350°F (180°C) mark 4 and continue cooking for a further

1¼ hours. The duck and pork will then serve eight people.

COOKING

Duck is usually roasted and served with a stuffing and a sauce.

Roasting

Preparation
Remember to completely thaw a frozen duck before roasting. It may be stuffed but it does tend to get rather greasy, so it is better to cook the stuffing separately in a dish. Truss the bird with small skewers or string and place on a rack in a roasting tin. Season with salt and prick the skin with a fork. As duck is very fatty, it is not necessary to brush the skin with any fat, nor to cover it with foil unless it is browning too quickly while cooking. Roast, basting occasionally, according to the details below.

To test that the duck is cooked
Pierce the thickest part of the thigh with a fine skewer; if clear juices run out, the duck is cooked. If the juices are slightly pink-tinged, continue cooking until they are clear. After cooking, cover the duck with foil, keep warm in the oven and allow it to 'rest' for 10 minutes before carving (see facing page).

Roasting times

Approximate weight of duck	Oven temperature	Approximate cooking time
3 lb (1.4kg)	350°F (180°C) mark 4	1 hour 40 minutes
4 lb (1.8kg)	350°F (180°C) mark 4	2 hours 10 minutes
5 lb (2.3kg)	350°F (180°C) mark 4	2 hours 30 minutes
6 lb (2.7kg)	350°F (180°C) mark 4	3 hours

Roasting times

Approximate weight of goose	Oven temperature	Approximate cooking time
8 lb (3.6kg)	400°F (200°C) mark 6 for the first hour of cooking time,	2 hours 40 minutes
10 lb (4.5kg)	then reduce the oven temperature to 350°F (180°C) mark 4 for the	3 hours 20 minutes
12 lb (4.7kg)	remaining cooking time	3 hours 40 minutes

Goose

Goose is at its best from October to Christmas. It has a fairly shallow breast with comparatively little flesh in proportion to its size and weight.

How much to buy

A 10 lb (4.5kg) oven-ready bird will serve eight.

COOKING

Goose is usually roasted and served with a stuffing and a sauce.

Roasting

Remember to completely thaw a frozen goose before roasting. A goose may be stuffed but it does tend to get rather greasy, so it is better to cook the stuffing separately in a dish. Truss the bird with small skewers or string and place on a rack in a roasting tin. Season with salt and prick the skin with a fork. As goose is very fatty, it is not necessary to brush the skin with any fat, nor to cover it with foil unless it is browning too quickly while cooking. Roast, basting occasionally, according to the details above.

To test that the goose is cooked
Pierce the thickest part of the leg with a fine skewer; if clear juices run out, the goose is cooked. If the juices are slightly pink-tinged, continue cooking until they are clear. After cooking, cover the goose with foil, keep warm in the oven and allow it to 'rest' for about 10 minutes before carving.

The principles of carving poultry are simple, and apply to most birds.

1 After cooking, allow the bird to 'rest' for about 10 minutes before carving to make the flesh firmer and easier to carve. Remove any string.
2 Carve on a flat, slip-proof surface such as a wooden board, using a sharp knife and a fork with a safety guard.
3 If carving a whole bird, remove the legs first, then the wings, then carve the breast in thin slices. If carving only a few portions, carve from one side of the bird only.

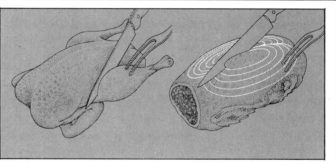

GOOSE
Carve with the breast uppermost. If carving the whole bird, first remove the legs (left), then the wings. If the bird is stuffed, cut thick slices across the body from the neck end. Carve thickish slices from either side of the breastbone (right).

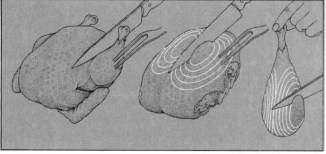

CHICKEN
Carve with the breast uppermost. If carving the whole bird, first remove the legs (left), then the wings. Carve thin slices from either side of the breastbone (centre). If the chicken is large, carve in the same way as turkey.
TURKEY
Carve with the breast uppermost. If carving the whole bird, first remove the drumsticks (lower part of the leg), leaving the thighs on the bird. Firmly hold the exposed knuckle end of the drumstick and carve in downward slices (right). Carve slices from the thighs, then remove the wings. Carve thin slices from either side of the breastbone (centre).

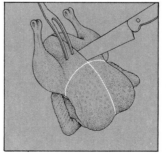

DUCK
Carve with the breast uppermost. Beginning at the neck end, use a sharp knife, kitchen scissors or poultry shears to cut along the length of the breastbone. Split the duck in half by cutting through the backbone. Make a diagonal cut between the wings and legs to give four portions.

A GUIDE TO

OFFAL

Offal to most people means liver and kidney and perhaps heart. But there is a lot more to offal than that. There are heads and tails, tripe and brains, tongues and cheeks. Offal is relatively inexpensive and is certainly nourishing, but it *must* be eaten fresh. Buy only as much as you need and use it on the same day; don't keep it in the refrigerator for more than 24 hours.

Liver

When you buy liver, it should be smooth and glossy. Buy it in one piece or ask your butcher to slice it for you. Soak it for an hour in cold salted water before cooking, then be sure to remove all the veins and outside skin. Liver should never be overcooked.

Calf's liver is the best and most expensive and is both tender and delicately flavoured. Fry or grill it and serve with onion gravy (see page 59). Lamb's liver is less expensive, mild in flavour and perfect for general family recipes. Pig's liver has a stronger flavour which some people dislike. Some of the strong flavour can be removed by soaking the liver in milk for a few hours. It is excellent in pâtés, meat loaves or stews. Ox liver is the cheapest and the coarsest. It is not suitable for grilling or frying but can be braised or stewed.

Kidneys

Remove the skin and core (the latter is most easily done with sharp kitchen scissors) before cooking kidneys.

Ox kidneys are the cheapest and have the strongest flavour. Since they need long, slow cooking, they are best used in stews and in steak and kidney pies or puddings. Calf's kidneys are more tender and also benefit from long, slow cooking. Lamb's kidneys are best for grilling or frying or they can be served in a sauce. Pig's kidneys, like pig's liver, have a stronger flavour. They can be cut in half lengthwise and grilled or chopped up and used in stews and risottos.

Heart

Heart is a strong muscle which must be carefully cooked if it is not to be tough and dry. It needs a strongly flavoured stuffing and is improved by a sharp sauce. Choose a heart that is a good red colour and allow about 6-10 oz (175-275g) per portion, depending on the amount of stuffing used. Both lambs' and pigs' hearts are more tender than ox heart and are usually stuffed, then roasted or braised. Calves' and lambs' hearts can be cut in slices and sautéed. They can be tenderised by marinating for 30 minutes in olive oil and lemon juice before cooking.

Heads

It is essential that heads are cleaned and blanched before cooking. Ox cheek must be stewed or casseroled very slowly indeed, but it makes an economical dish with a fine flavour. Calf's head is usually sold already boned and blanched. It can be boiled, made into a brawn, or added to jellied veal. The rich, gelatinous meat is easily digested. It is good served cold with vinaigrette or sliced, then fried or grilled. Sheep's head is boiled for broth, the meat being served separately. Pig's head is boiled to make brawn.

Feet

Cow heel should be boiled or stewed. Calf's feet make a nourishing jelly which was formerly given to invalids but which is now cooked with other meats to make brawn and enrich meat dishes. Pig's trotters may be boiled or stewed, then fried or grilled. They can be added to brawn.

Tongues

When buying tongue, make sure that the skin is smooth; a rough skin is an indication of age. Salted and smoked tongue is best soaked overnight before cooking. Carving a tongue is important to its flavour: never cut it in cubes but in the thinnest-possible slices. Hot tongue should be carved in long slices about ¼ in. (0.6cm) thick.

Ox tongue has a good flavour and a pleasant texture and is sold fresh, salted and sometimes smoked. Calves' tongues are very delicate in flavour and are usually sold fresh. Sheep tongues are smaller and, like calves' tongues, are usually poached or braised and served cold, or hot with sauce.

Calf's sweetbreads

Lamb's sweetbreads

Pig's brains

Ox sweetbreads

Ox brains

Calf's brains

Lamb's brains

Ox liver

Ox heart

Oxtail

Ox cheek

Lamb's liver

Pig's liver

Haggis

Lambs' hearts

Calf's liver

Ox kidneys

Ox tongue

Pig's trotters

Pigs' kidneys

Calves' tongues

Lambs' kidneys

Lambs' tongues

Tripe

Sweetbreads

These must be bought when they are really fresh and should be used at once. Ox sweetbreads are the cheapest but they must be cooked very slowly to make them tender. Calf's sweetbreads are more expensive, but the best, tenderest and most expensive of all are lamb's sweetbreads. Allow one pair per portion and keep them as white as possible by soaking them for at least four hours in cold water which should be changed several times. Put them in cold salted water and bring to the boil. Remove the veins and skin, place the blanched sweetbreads between two plates to flatten them and allow to cool. They can then be coated with egg and breadcrumbs and sautéed in butter.

Tripe

Tripe comes from the stomach lining of an ox. It is a light, easily digested meat that must be prepared carefully. It is sold already cleaned and blanched, but it requires further cooking. It need not be the greyish stew of popular belief: try it fried with onions or sliced and simmered in a spicy sauce.

Brains

These should be bought when they are really fresh and used as soon as possible after purchase. Calf's brains should be soaked in cold water for 15 minutes before blanching and removing the membrane. They may be poached and served with a sauce or may be served with a calf's head. Two sets of brains will provide enough to serve three people. Lamb's brains are usually cooked with the head but can be served separately. Allow one or two sets per portion.

Oxtail

This makes delicious well-flavoured stews or soups. One large oxtail will usually provide enough meat for six portions. Oxtail is inclined to be fatty so remove all excess fat before cooking, then skim off the fat again when the tail is cooked. It is necessary to cook oxtail for a long time because the meat is tough, but it has a delicious flavour.

GAME

Game birds and animals live mainly in the wild and their feeding habits depend on the food available to them in their native countryside. Consequently their flavour is unique and individual. Game, with few exceptions, is very strictly protected in Britain and is obtainable only at certain times of the year. A butcher needs a special licence to deal in it.

All game, except water birds such as wild duck, must be hung; this is essential to make the meat tender. The time for which it must be hung varies according to taste (some people like their game very well hung), the type of game and the weather. Naturally it must be hung for a longer period if the weather is really cold, but a shorter time will do in hot weather. It should be plucked and drawn after hanging – never before – and immediately before it is to be cooked.

Game keeps well in the freezer, but it must be hung first; it must never be hung after freezing. Ideally a bird should be plucked before it is put in the freezer but, if absolutely necessary, it may be hung and put in the freezer in feather, then plucked when partially thawed and drawn when completely thawed. When freezing, it is wise to separate and label young and older birds so that, when you come to use them, you know which are for roasting and which for casseroling. Freeze in a thick polythene bag from which air has been excluded. Thaw overnight in the refrigerator for a small bird, or two days for a larger bird.

Cook game as you would any other meat. Only tender young birds or animals should be roasted, while others can be braised, casseroled, or used in pies and terrines.

Pheasant

This is in season from 1 October to 1 February. Pheasants are sold in pairs known as a brace i.e. a cock and a hen. The cock bird is usually larger while the hen is fatter and more tender. A brace serves six to eight portions. Hang birds in feather from the neck for about a week, depending on the weather, in a very cool, draughty larder or outhouse which should be fly-proof if possible. Keep them out of reach of domestic pets. If you are freezing several pheasants, keep the livers and freeze them separately. They can then be mixed with chicken livers and made into a pâté, using about one-third pheasant livers to two-thirds chicken livers.

Remove any excess yellow fat from the pheasants. Lightly spread the birds with butter and season with salt and freshly ground black pepper. Place pieces of fat bacon or bacon rinds on the breast and roast in the oven at 400°F (200°C) mark 6 for about 50 minutes. After about 25 minutes, remove the bacon and baste the birds.

Make a gravy using the juices (see page 58), adding redcurrant jelly and a dash of port, Madeira or fortified wine. Serve with bacon rolls, fried breadcrumbs (fresh white breadcrumbs which have been fried in butter and oil until pale brown, then seasoned), game chips, bread sauce (see page 58) and a fruit jelly such as redcurrant or apple.

Grouse

This is in season from 12 August to 10 December. Allow one young grouse per person: a larger, more mature bird will serve two. Hang the birds for about three days, as detailed for pheasant.

Roast grouse in the same way as pheasant, but reduce the cooking time to about 30 minutes if the birds are small. As soon as they are cooked, slip each grouse onto a croûte of crustless bread that has been fried in butter. (The cooked liver may be mashed with a little butter, salt and freshly ground black pepper, then spread on the fried bread before the bird is placed on top.) In this way the juices from the bird drip through onto the fried bread. No other accompaniments are necessary, except thin gravy, redcurrant or fruit jelly and perhaps some fresh, chopped parsley. Older birds need to be casseroled.

Ptarmigan

This is in season from 12 August to 10 December, but is quite difficult to obtain. It is very similar to a grouse, though is not considered to have such a good flavour. Allow one bird per person. Cook and serve in the same way as grouse.

Blackcock

This is in season from 20 August to 10 December, but is quite difficult to obtain. It is a less common kind of grouse and the hen of the species is known

Red legged partridge

English partridge

Hare

Rabbit

Guinea fowl

Wild duck (male)

Red legged partridge, dressed

Wood pigeon

Grouse

Venison

English partridge, dressed

Wood pigeon, dressed

Brace of pheasants

Hen pheasant

Wild duck (female)

Cock pheasant

Guinea fowl, dressed

Pheasant, dressed

Woodcock

E.C. DAWSON & SON

HALESWORTH

as a greyhen. Prepare in the same way as grouse but, as the flesh is inclined to be dry, add more butter. Cook and serve in the same way as grouse, but increase the cooking time by about 5 minutes.

Partridge

This is in season from 1 September to 1 February. English partridge is preferable to the red legged or French variety. In Britain the latter are now reared for the table rather than for a shoot, which means that the eggs are hatched and the birds reared on farms rather than living in the wild and being shot eventually. As a result they tend to lack flavour but are guaranteed to be tender. Allow one bird per person. Hang the birds for three to four days, as detailed for pheasant. Roast in the same way as pheasant, but reduce the cooking time to 30 minutes. Serve in the same way as pheasant. Older birds should be casseroled.

Wild duck

This is in season from 1 September to 31 January or, under certain conditions, until 28 February. If the duck is a mallard, allow one bird for two people; some kinds will serve only one. Roast in the oven at 350°F (180°C) mark 4 for about 1 hour, basting frequently. Do not overcook. Serve with thin gravy (see page 58) mixed with orange juice, redcurrant jelly mixed with port and orange salad.

Wild goose

This is in season from 1 September to 20 February on the foreshore and from 1 September to 31 January inland. These are usually Canadian geese and can taste slightly fishy if they have come from a salt marsh area. They may be older birds, so always cook them slowly as they are fairly lean, quite unlike domestic geese. An 8 lb (3.6kg) bird will serve eight people. Place the goose on a rack in a roasting tin, place a bunch of herbs and a little chopped onion inside the bird and brush the skin with butter. Roast in the oven at 425°F (220°C) mark 7 for about 30 minutes or until the breast is browned. Reduce the oven temperature to 300°F (150°C) mark 2 and continue roasting for a further 30 minutes per lb (450g). Baste occasionally and cover loosely with foil for the last half of the cooking time. Serve with thin gravy (see page 58), orange salad, redcurrant or rowan jelly and garnish with watercress.

Venison

Venison is now more widely available and the best roasting cuts are the haunch, loin and saddle. Venison must be hung for eight to ten days before cooking and is improved by marinating. The meat is very dry so bacon rashers should be tied to it before cooking. Roast in the oven at 375°F (190°C) mark 5, allowing 30 minutes per lb (450g). Serve with redcurrant, rowan or cranberry jelly or Cumberland sauce (see page 58). Venison is also very good casseroled with onions, particularly if you are given a piece as a present and you can't distinguish which part of the animal it is. Stewing venison is exceptionally good and may be casseroled with wine or beer. I once used it in a recipe for jugged hare instead of hare, and it was superb.

Wood pigeon

This is available throughout the year. There is no need to hang the birds. Only young birds should be roasted; older ones can be casseroled. Allow one young pigeon per person; a larger, older bird will serve two. Roast pigeon in the same way as pheasant, but reduce the cooking time to 30 minutes.

Woodcock

This is in season from 1 October to 31 January. Hang for about three days, as detailed for pheasant. Allow at least one bird per person. Cook and serve in the same way as grouse, but do not draw the bird, and reduce the cooking time to 20 minutes.

Snipe

This is in season from 12 August to 31 January, but is quite difficult to obtain. Hang for about three days, as detailed for pheasant. Allow at least one bird per person. Cook and serve in the same way as grouse, but do not draw the bird, and reduce the cooking time to 20 minutes.

Quail

This is a migratory bird and is therefore available only in the summer if killed in its natural habitat. However, they are now bred commercially and are available from some poulterers. Quail should be eaten soon after it is killed. Allow one bird per person. Cook and serve in the same way as grouse, but reduce the cooking time to 15-20 minutes.

Guinea fowl

This is no longer regarded as game. A bird weighs about 2½-3 lb (1.1-1.4kg) and will provide enough for three or four portions. It should be hung for about five days, as detailed for pheasant, and roasted in the same way as chicken (see page 29).

Rabbit

This is in season throughout the year but wild rabbits are at their best from September to February. A whole young rabbit provides four portions and is very good if made into rabbit pie. Rabbit can also be cooked in the same way as chicken (see page 29) but should be soaked in salted water for an hour before cooking to improve the flavour.

Hare

There is no closed season but it is illegal to sell hare in the shops between March and July. Hang for about a week, as detailed for pheasant. Hare can be roasted but is inclined to be dry, so it is better if jugged (see page 202).

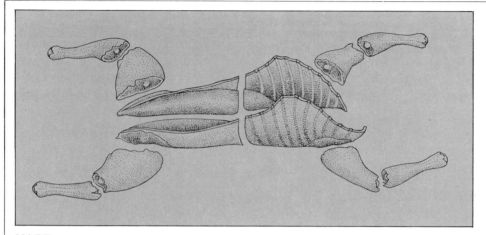

HARE

A hare is normally already jointed when you buy it. If, however, you are given one as a present, skin and paunch it, then joint it as follows. Cut off the skin flaps below the rib cage. Cut the body in half lengthwise along the the backbone, then make a cut across the body to give four sections. If the hare is large, the body can be divided into more sections. Remove the fore legs at the shoulder, then cut each leg into two, chopping through the bone. Remove the hind legs at the thigh, then cut into two, chopping through the bone.

A GUIDE TO
VEAL

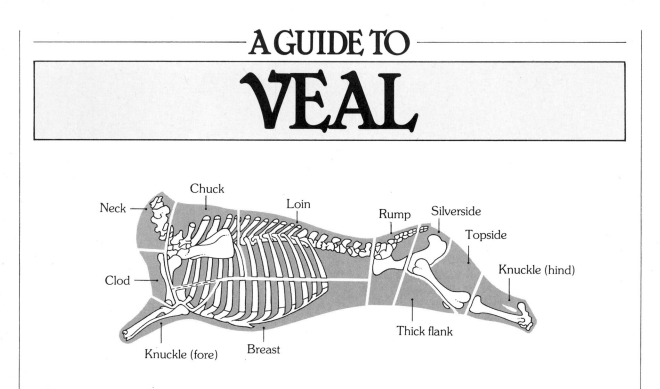

Neck · Chuck · Loin · Rump · Silverside · Topside · Knuckle (hind)
Clod · Knuckle (fore) · Breast · Thick flank

BUYING

Very little veal is eaten in Britain; in fact, it accounts for only four per cent of all meat consumed, and most of that goes into the catering trade. Two kinds of veal are available: one is meat from a calf fed only on milk and the other from a grass-fed calf. Milk-fed veal is very tender, very expensive and most of it is imported. The grass-fed variety is not so tender but it is often considered to have the better flavour. Veal does not keep very well and, since the demand for it is so small, many butchers are reluctant to stock it.

What to look for

The flesh should be soft, moist and very pale pink. There is little fat, except around the kidneys, and no gristle, but a gelatinous connective tissue instead which softens easily when cooked. The bones are pinkish-white and soft and produce a great deal of jelly when boiled. Veal cooks much more quickly than beef, being a younger animal.

How much to buy

As a guide, allow 8–12 oz (225–350g) per portion for veal on the bone; 4–6 oz (100–150g) for boned and rolled veal; one escalope per portion for veal chops.

COOKING

Roasting

Veal is inclined to be a dry meat and is often better suited to braising than to roasting, although a moist stuffing and careful basting can do a lot to improve

Roasting times

Approximate weight of veal joint	Oven temperature	Approximate cooking time
1 lb (450g)	400°F (200°C) mark 6	1 hour 10 minutes
2 lb (900g)	400°F (200°C) mark 6	1 hour 30 minutes
3 lb (1.4kg)	400°F (200°C) mark 6	2 hours
4 lb (1.8kg)	400°F (200°C) mark 6	2 hours 20 minutes
Over 4 lb (1.8kg)	400°F (200°C) mark 6	20 minutes per lb (450g)

Breast

Loin – boned and rolled

Cutlet chops

Loin chops

Bones

Pie veal

Whole knuckle

Escalopes (from rump) – unbeaten

Neck

Knuckle – cut into pieces

Oyster (from shoulder)

Escalopes (from rump) – beaten

the quality of a roast. Veal joints are not widely available for roasting but, if they are, they are usually boned and rolled.

Preparation

Lightly spread with butter or chicken fat and season well with salt and freshly ground black pepper. Place the joint on a rack in a roasting tin and cook, basting occasionally, according to the details on the previous page. When the meat is brown, cover with foil to prevent it from drying out during cooking.

To test that the veal is cooked

Pierce the thickest part of the joint with a fine skewer; if clear juices run out, the meat·is cooked. If the juices are slightly pink-tinged, continue cooking until they are clear.

Grilling and frying

See the methods given for beef (page 13).

Suitable cuts: Chops, escalopes (thin, filleted slices cut from the top of the leg or from the under part of the loin).

Braising and pot roasting

See the methods given for beef (pages 12 and 13).

Suitable cuts: Boned shoulder, chops, breast (boned, rolled and stuffed).

Stews and casseroles

See the methods given for beef (page 13).

Suitable cuts: Neck, breast, shoulder, knuckle, hock.

Pies

Use pie veal which comes from the shoulder, neck and breast.

CARVING

Veal should be carved in moderately thick slices. After cooking, cover the joint with foil or a large heatproof dish or basin, keep warm in the oven and allow it to 'rest' for about 10 minutes before carving.

LEFT-OVERS

Cold roast veal is delicious with salads and pickles, or can be used to make a fricassée which must be seasoned well.

FREEZING MEAT

The domestic freezer is responsible for one of the biggest household revolutions of our time, particularly in our attitude to the buying and storing of meat. At one time, foods were bought only as and when they were needed, and were cooked and eaten on the same day. This probably entailed a visit to the butcher two or three times a week. Today, the owner of a freezer can buy meat in bulk – perhaps a forequarter or hindquarter of beef, or a side of lamb or pork. These can be divided into different cuts by the butcher, who will then package them ready for freezing. Stews, casseroles and pies can be prepared from the cheaper cuts and then stored, either cooked or uncooked, in the freezer. Nothing is wasted.

Money can be saved in several ways by bulk buying. Meat can be bought when it is plentiful and the price is lower; a bulk purchase may be shared among two or more families; all parts of a carcass can be used; and, above all, there is always a store of meat on hand when it is wanted. Your own butcher may very well give you a discount if you buy meat in bulk from him.

What is freezing?

Briefly, it is the simplest and most natural way of preserving food which, if properly frozen, can be kept safely for long periods. A domestic freezer stores food at a temperature of 0°F (−18°C) and is capable of reducing to this temperature a specified quantity of fresh food (see manufacturer's recommendations) within 24 hours, without affecting the quality or storage life of food already in the freezer. This is what distinguishes a freezer from the ordinary food storage compartment of a refrigerator. The symbol of a large six-pointed star followed by three small stars indicates the freezer's ability to freeze as well as to store frozen food.

Meat of all kinds can therefore be safely frozen and stored. Offal, for example, which keeps fresh for only 24 hours in the refrigerator and should be eaten on the day of purchase, can be stored for up to three months in a freezer without any deterioration in quality.

Buying for the freezer

Always buy the best quality meat available. A supply of meat for the freezer can be a considerable capital investment, so it makes sense to get the best possible value for money by buying the best quality meat.

Choose your supplier with care. A reliable butcher will cut and pack to your requirements and should be ready to advise you on your purchases. Supermarkets often supply meat for home freezing but, if you do not want to freeze your own, cash-and-carry supermarkets and freezer food centres offer ready cut, packed and frozen carcasses, sides or quarters, in addition to packs of joints, steaks, chops. mince and offal.

If you are buying in bulk from your butcher, it is as well to order from him well in advance. This gives him time to prepare and hang the meat (a skilled job which must be left to the butcher) in order that it develops flavour and tenderness. You can buy and freeze sides or quarters of beef, lamb or pork carcasses, or a selection of your family's favourite cuts from these. Salt beef, ham or bacon should not be frozen in quantity as their storage life is short. Buy these in small quantities and use them quickly.

When freezing chickens, choose plump, tender young birds only. Older, tougher birds should be cooked or their meat made into pies or casseroles before they are frozen. All poultry and game freezes well but do remember that game must be hung before freezing.

When to buy

The price of meat is subject to seasonal fluctuation and consumer demand. It is sensible to watch for special offers on quarters of beef or lamb, on lamb or pork carcasses, or on special cuts of meat. It is also useful to make a note of the times of peak supply. Beef is most plentiful, and consequently at its cheapest, in late summer and early autumn. Although pork is available throughout the year, there tends to be less demand for it in hot weather and this is a good time to buy in bulk. It freezes well in both its raw state and in made-up dishes. English lamb is expensive early in the season, from March onwards, while prices fall in late summer and autumn. Stewing cuts of meat are usually cheaper in the summer, too.

Stocking the freezer

The secret here is organisation. It is no good having a freezer full of food if you can't tell the package of mince you put in a couple of weeks ago from the parcel of steaks that have been there for three months. Clearly label each package (see notes on packing materials below) and keep a written record of what is put in the freezer. It is important to make a note of dates in order that food can be used in rotation so there is a steady turnover in the freezer.

Keep the same kinds of meat together: joints in one compartment or basket, smaller cuts and minced meat in another, offal in a third, and a section for poultry and game. Use wire baskets to make the removal of food a simple matter, and you won't have to unpack the whole freezer to find that elusive packet of chops that you know is in there somewhere. If you have frozen a large, heavy item such as a turkey which you won't be using for some months, put it at the bottom of a chest freezer or at the back of an upright one so that you won't have to keep lifting it out every time you are looking for something.

Try to pack the containers as close together as possible. A well-packed freezer is more economical to run than one in which there is room for air circulation between awkwardly shaped packages.

Careful packaging keeps meat in good condition; if it is not well wrapped, it can deteriorate rapidly. The condition known as 'freezer-burn' is the result of inadequate wrapping. Meat suffering from freezer-burn becomes dehydrated and loses some of its texture and flavour, while acquiring unsightly greyish marks. Although it is perfectly safe to eat, it will tend to be dry and flavourless.

Packing materials suitable for freezing meat include:

■ Double aluminium foil (or use one layer of foil, then slip the package into an old, clean polythene bag). This can be wrapped closely round meat, thereby excluding as much air as possible, and needs no special sealing.

■ Extra-thick polythene bags or rigid polythene containers.

■ Freezer cling film or polythene sheets to interleave chops, steaks and sausages to make separation easy. Pack in polythene bags.

■ Wire ties or freezer tape to secure the packages.

■ Labels are essential if you are not to lose track of the contents of the freezer. Label each package boldly with a waterproof marker, stating what it contains, how many it will serve (or the weight, if raw meat) and the date it was put in the freezer. Packages should be dated so they can be used in rotation.

■ A notebook is necessary so that you can keep a written record of what's in the freezer.

Packing meat

Make sure that all utensils and work surfaces are scrupulously clean before you start. Cut off excess fat from joints, steaks and chops as it wastes valuable freezer space. Tie joints into neat shapes and truss poultry ready for cooking. Pad any sharp bones or points of skewers with polythene or foil. Minced meat can be divided into convenient amounts. Pack these in foil or in polythene bags and press into rectangular shapes so they will fit together in the minimum amount of space. Offal should be divided into convenient amounts immediately after purchase. It is better to freeze stuffings separately rather than in the meat or bird.

Cooked meat and prepared dishes

The freezer owner can always have available a stock of ready-cooked dishes which need only be thawed and heated in the oven before serving. The busy mother can have a supply of favourite family meals on hand; the hostess can freeze dishes ready for dinner parties; and housewives can set a day aside to prepare casseroles, stews, pies, potted meats, terrines, soups and sauces to go into the freezer. These can be used as required with no last-minute dashes or long hours in the kitchen when guests are expected. If you set time aside to prepare a supply of dishes to be frozen in bulk, you will also be saving money on fuel because several dishes can be cooked in the oven at the same time.

When you are storing ready-prepared dishes, try to achieve square or rectangular packs in order to save space. For example, 4 lb (1.8kg) of cooked minced beef can be packed in a roasting tin and cut into four before it is fully frozen. When it has frozen completely, it can be removed from the tin, packed in freezer wrap and stored in the freezer. A casserole or stew, which should not be overcooked, can be frozen in the dish in which it was cooked. When frozen, dip the dish in hot water and turn out the contents like a jelly, then pack in freezer wrap and store. The dish can then be used for cooking other foods, while the stored package is the right shape to put back into the dish for thawing and heating when you are ready to serve it. I do this with lasagne and moussaka. Alternatively, you can line the dish with foil before cooking so the contents can be easily removed for freezing.

Storage times

It should be made clear from the start that it is perfectly safe to eat meat which has been kept in the freezer after the recommended storage time. Food poisoning bacteria cannot multiply on properly frozen food, so they cannot become a health hazard no matter how long the meat is kept. The danger arises when the frozen food is thawed and kept in a warmer temperature for too long. However, it cannot be denied that the flavour and appearance of all frozen food does deteriorate if it is kept in store too long.

At a constant temperature of 0°F (−18°C) or below, meat has a reasonably long storage life. This is largely determined by the fat content. Pig fat turns rancid more quickly than the fat of beef or lamb, and the presence of salt accelerates the change. Bacon and dishes containing pork fat therefore have a shorter storage life than other foods, although vacuum-packing considerably extends the storage time for bacon and ham joints.

Recommended storage times
For freezers operating at 0°F (−18°C)

Uncooked meat	Months
Beef	12
Mince	3
Sausages	3
Lamb	9
Pork	6
Bacon joints	3
Bacon joints (vacuum-packed)	4
Bacon rashers, chops and gammon steaks	1
Bacon rashers, chops and gammon steaks (vacuum-packed)	3
Chicken	12
Turkey	12
Duck	6
Offal	3
Game	12
Veal	9

Cooked meat	Months
Joints	3
Ham	2
Casseroles (with bacon)	3
Casseroles (without bacon)	6
Curry	4
Meat pies	1
Sliced meat (with gravy)	3
Sliced meat (without gravy)	2
Shepherd's pie	3
Soup	3

Thawing meat

The best and safest way to thaw frozen meat is in the refrigerator, where it should be placed one or two days before it is required. It can of course be thawed more quickly at room temperature, or even more quickly in a microwave oven. When thawing it must be kept free from contamination and must be cooked thoroughly as soon as possible.

It is advisable to thaw all joints before cooking, but small cuts such as steaks, chops, liver, kidneys and meat for stews and kebabs may be satisfactorily cooked from the frozen state. In this case it is necessary to double the cooking time given in a recipe. Start cooking at a low temperature and increase the heat halfway through the cooking time.

It is essential to completely thaw boned and rolled joints, whether stuffed or unstuffed. The inner and outer surfaces of these joints have been handled, and therefore thorough cooking is necessary to destroy any bacteria that may be present.

It cannot be stressed too often that all frozen poultry on the bone must be completely thawed before it is cooked. This is to ensure that sufficient heat penetrates the flesh to destroy any bacteria. Stuffing should be frozen separately. Poultry should be kept in a refrigerator when it has thawed.

Frozen raw meat may be thawed, then cooked and re-frozen perfectly safely. Cool the cooked meat quickly in the refrigerator before putting it back in the freezer.

KITCHEN EQUIPMENT

All the best and most professional cooks have their favourite tools, old friends of many years' service, which have been carefully chosen, polished and sharpened and are always to hand. In recent years, advances in the field of electrical kitchen equipment have added a whole new dimension to the preparation and cooking of food. Food processors, mixers, blenders, microwave ovens, infra-red grills, slow cooking pots, deep-fat fryers, sandwich toasters: all have been developed to take the drudgery out of cooking and to save time.

It would be easy enough – and great fun – to spend a small fortune on kitting out a kitchen, but do think carefully before you buy, and choose equipment that is best suited to your needs. Do you entertain at home a great deal, and therefore require a large battery of saucepans? Are you a working woman who is best served by a slow cooker which can take care of a stew while you are out, or a fast grill that will produce a quick meal in minutes on your return? Is your kitchen large or small? What sort of preparation space do you have? And, most important of all, what are you going to cook?

CUTTING TOOLS

Knives

Good knives are essential for meat cookery so don't economise on these. One expensive knife that can be kept really sharp is worth any number of cheap ones and, with care, will last a lifetime.

Cook's knives

A cook's knife is used on raw meat, and a good one is well balanced, easy to handle, and makes cutting and chopping meat a pleasure rather than a chore. The handle should fit comfortably in the hand, and a carbon or stainless steel blade is easily sharpened.

Carving knives

While cook's knives are of fairly rugged construction, carving knives, for cooked meat, are more flexible. Pointed knives are used for carving joints on the bone, while those intended for cold meats or ham have long, narrow blades.

Knife sharpeners

Whatever kind of knife you use, keep it sharp. Professionals use a sharpening steel, but learning to use one effectively requires some practice. There are various knife sharpeners on the market which are easy and safe to use. Electric sharpeners are available too.

Cutting boards

Never cut or chop on a hard surface such as ceramic, metal or plastic; always use a wooden chopping or slicing board which will not damage the knife blade. For the dining table carving boards are available, which ideally should have a channel to catch the meat juices.

OTHER SMALL TOOLS

Spoons and ladles

Slotted metal spoons are used for lifting meat out of a pan while leaving behind the gravy or juices. Ladles are useful for serving stews and sauces. Wooden spoons are for stirring stews, sauces and gravies, though I prefer to use wooden spatulas with straight flat bases so that all corners of the pan can be reached. Tongs are available for lifting and turning too. Metal utensils should not be used on non-stick surfaces.

Forks

These hold joints or poultry steady when carving. I consider a guard on the fork to be essential for safety, in order that the hand is protected from accidental slips of the knife.

Scissors

Good sharp scissors are invaluable for trimming meat, cutting small poultry joints, removing bacon rind from rashers, or cutting the cores from kidneys.

Mincers

Mincers, like food processors (see right), save a lot of time, trouble and energy which would otherwise be spent in chopping meat with a knife. They come in different shapes and sizes, but buy the best you can afford. A good mincer will work quickly and efficiently and is ideal for dealing with left-over cooked meat. Trim off all bone, gristle, rind and most of the fat from the meat to be minced and feed the meat into the machine, a little at a time. At the end of each batch to be minced, clean out the machine by mincing a lump of bread, which also helps to thicken the mince.

Meat thermometers

A meat thermometer is fitted with a thin probe which is pushed into a joint of meat to indicate the temperature inside, and is useful if you lack confidence in deciding when a joint is cooked. It pays to buy a reputable make as cheap ones are rarely accurate. Although meat thermometers may seem a good idea, they haven't proved particularly popular in Britain.

Roasting bags

These are made of a strong special type of plastic and should be big enough to hold a whole joint or bird. They help to keep the meat moist and prevent fat from splashing the inside of the oven.

ELECTRICAL APPLIANCES

All these appliances - and there is an enormous variety on the market - have one thing in common: a small electric motor which drives blades, shredders and beaters at high speed. They are expensive, of course, and you need space for them in the kitchen, but they speed up and simplify the preparation of food for the family, for the freezer or for entertaining.

Blenders and liquidisers

These usually consist of the base containing the electric motor and a goblet in which the food is prepared, and are sometimes attached to a mixer. They chop nuts, make breadcrumbs and prepare purées, soups, baby foods, sauces, drinks and batters. Some will chop cooked meat, and will most efficiently purée raw liver for pâtés if liquid is added.

Hand-held mixers

These whip eggs and cream, beat omelettes and mix batters, and some will cream cake mixtures and knead bread dough too. They are portable and easy to use.

Table mixers

These are more expensive, more powerful, and take up more room in the kitchen than the hand-held variety, but they do a great deal more work. The various optional attachments available make them extremely versatile.

Food processors

These are a fairly new development as far as the domestic kitchen is concerned. Simple to use, speedy and compact, the food processor may well be more effective than the table mixer in the preparation of meat and vegetables. Basically, the machine consists of a powerful and silent motor which very quickly turns a sharp, double-bladed knife in a plastic bowl. It takes about 15 seconds to mince meat, while puréeing can be done in about 20 seconds. Most models have discs for slicing or shredding, but no other extras are necessary.

COOKING EQUIPMENT

Saucepans

A set of good saucepans will last a lifetime so don't buy cheap ones. The best pans are made of metals that are good heat conductors such as cast iron, stainless steel, aluminium or copper. Aluminium is one of the least expensive and most commonly used and aluminium pans will be satisfactory if they are heavy and the bases are ground. Enamelled cast iron pans are good for distributing heat evenly and will last well if treated with care. Stainless steel pans are the easiest to keep sparkling. Pan lids should fit well and the handles should be heatproof and easy to hold. The base of a pan should be thick and smooth so that the heat is evenly distributed.

Casseroles

These are heavy, lidded pots which may be made of enamelled cast iron or earthenware and can be used either in the oven or on the hob. They are ideal for stews and other meat dishes that require long, slow cooking.

Pressure cookers

A pressure cooker will cook in half the time any food that is normally steamed, boiled or stewed, and is invaluable for dealing with the tougher cuts of meat.

Roasting tins

Roasting tins for meat and poultry are usually shallow and have flat bases. Deeper tins with lids can produce a moister joint and will prevent fat from splashing the inside of the oven. Whatever type you buy, choose one that will be easy to lift from a hot oven. Always use a small tin for a small joint. A rack or grid that fits in the bottom of the roasting tin is very useful, and ensures that the joint doesn't sit in fat while it's cooking.

Contact grills (infra-red grills)

A contact grill is useful for all grilling and frying of meats, and consists of two non-stick plates between which the meat is placed. It is heated by infra-red radiation which penetrates food more quickly than heat from conventional electric elements. Some manufacturers state that these grills can be used to cook meat straight from the freezer, but I prefer to thaw mine first.

Microwave ovens

Cooking with one of these is very fast: about a quarter of the normal time. The oven can also be used for defrosting frozen food. A 2½ lb (1.1kg) roasting chicken can be taken from the freezer, thawed, cooked and ready to serve – all in under an hour, though don't expect it to be brown unless you have sprinkled it with special seasoning or you have a browning dish in the oven. A microwave oven is most useful for thawing and reheating foods.

Barbecues

Essentially an outdoor excercise. Basically, a barbecue consists of a metal box or tray to hold the charcoal fuel, over which is placed a grid to hold the steaks, chops or sausages to be grilled. Light the fire in plenty of time for it to become a glowing mass before the cooking starts. Also available are gas-fired barbecues, which are easy to use and highly efficient. Equipment for a barbecue comes in all shapes, sizes and prices.

Deep-fat fryers

Electric deep-fat fryers make cooking quick and easy. They also make deep-fat frying safer as they are thermostatically controlled and prevent the fat from getting too hot.

Sandwich toasters

These are fun to use for snack meals and provide a different way of using up the last piece of pâté or the last cuts from the Sunday roast. Toasted sandwiches prove popular with children of all ages.

Slow cookers

In contrast, the ultra-slow cooking pot will simmer food very, very gently – all day if necessary – so it is ideal for making stews and for cooking the cheaper cuts of meat.

Fondues

A fondue is a favourite form of party cooking at the table. For a meat fondue, oil is heated in a metal pan over a methylated spirit cooker, cubes of meat are skewered on long metal forks and are cooked in the oil by the guests. Various sauces and relishes are served, into which the meat is dipped. It is essential to use a tender cut of grilling meat for a fondue.

WINE WITH MEAT

It is widely assumed that, if you have enough money, there is no problem at all about choosing wine to go with any food; you simply buy the very best and you can't go wrong. But this is not necessarily the case. The 'right' wine can add an extra ingredient to the plainest dish while the wrong wine can fight a chef's masterpiece, and in that fight both wine and dish are losers - no matter how expensive the wine may be. The best way of finding out more about wine is to seek the advice of your local wine merchant. He will help you choose a wine suitable to accompany the food you are planning to serve, and will explain the characteristics of different wines which are now available from many countries. Visit him when his shop is not too busy, however: he may not appreciate you asking a lot of questions when he is trying to serve a number of other customers!

RED WINE

Almost the first thing any hostess planning a dinner party learns is to serve red wine with meat and white with fish. Not for nothing has this become one of the basic rules of serving wine. You can ignore such inherited lore only if you are very foolish - or very brave. However, this poses a question: should the red wine be claret or Burgundy? This question stems from another tradition concerning the serving of wine with meat, since it assumes that the only wine to be considered suitable should be French. This was once so, of course - and not so very long ago at that. If it were still so, however, the problems would remain, but the choice would be made relatively simple.

In some ways it is very tempting to uphold this tradition. Claret, meaning specifically red wine from the Bordeaux region of France, is best with uncomplicated meat dishes such as roast lamb, beef or veal, roast or braised poultry or cold dishes. Burgundy, meaning the red wines from the Rhône region further south, is best with pork, game and any casseroles containing herbs. This seems very simple, but is also rather expensive.

In the past, the wines that were usually recommended to serve with meat - a Château-bottled claret for its delicacy and a domaine-bottled Burgundy for its hint of power - are now frequently out of reach financially. But the problem is not insurmountable. As the great wines of France rocketed in price, so wines from hitherto unregarded areas of France and from other less 'fashionable' countries began to compete with them. Take, for instance, the red French regional wines from the south-west region between Toulouse and the foothills of the Pyrenees. These are the wines readily available from your wine merchant, local off-licence or supermarket, with labels indicating that they came from Hérault, or Corbières, or Roussillon: regions where vast quantities of everyday wine are produced and consumed. Much of it used to be, and indeed still can be, rather rough table wine. But now wine from this area, produced specifically for export, is vastly improved and consistent and, at half the price of claret, looks to be a ready-made substitute for which no one should feel obliged to apologise.

However, it should be remembered that, although these red wines are sold in high-necked, claret-style bottles and are sometimes marketed as though they were clarets, they are, in fact, wines in their own right with their own special qualities. Because they tend to be stronger and darker than clarets, they are often well-suited to the stronger, darker meats. For example, there is the red wine of Cohors which is so dark that it looks almost black by candlelight. It is excellent with a robust English dish such as steak and kidney pudding, or equally with a traditionally French dish such as cassoulet de porc. But I would not care to serve it with veal chops or a leg of lamb. To accompany such dishes - and ignoring the claims, on the grounds of price, of a lordly claret - a good choice would be a wine from northern Italy, such as Chianti Classico or a Valpolicella Superiore.

Barolo is an Italian wine which is certainly worth considering if you are seeking a wine to accompany a 'strong' meat dish and if you have decided that the price of a good Burgundy is too high. Along with Ghemme and Brunello di Montalcino, Barolo is one of the more expensive in the Italian price range, but all three are connoisseurs' wines obtainable at reasonable prices.

Across the Mediterranean, the wines of Spain are taking some time to recover from the stigma of being thought of as 'plonk'. But there are two wine-exporting areas of Spain which deserve to be

treated very seriously. One area is around Barcelona, variously called Panades or Penedes, which produces wine for those seeking a change from claret-style French wines. I have drunk Torres Coronas in Spain with cooked spicy sausage and in England with a Sunday joint. On both occasions it was most welcome. From the mountains of northern Spain come the red wines of Rioja, which are sometimes termed 'Burgundian' in style. In the sense that such wines as Rioja Carta de Oro or Vina Ardanza are 'meaty' wines, the term is acceptable; but it does not convey the special nature of the Rioja wines which, at three years of age, display remarkable maturity.

The most important consideration in the matter of choosing a wine to go with a particular dish is to ensure that the tastes of the wine and the meat don't clash. That is why the Greek Retsina, with its heavy taste of pine needles, sits so ill on the average dining table. There is no dish in the English cuisine with which Retsina will not fight to the death. It is for this reason that a heavy wine should not be served with veal or chicken and why it is a waste of money to serve a vintage claret with curry. Incidentally, what *should* be served with curry? If you feel you must offer some sort of wine, make it the cheapest and driest white you can find. Alternatively, stick to beer, preferably lager.

WHITE WINE

It is certainly possible to drink white wine with meat, although it depends very much on the meat and very much more on the wine. Never serve champagne throughout a meal. While it's quite true that champagne goes with almost any meal you are likely to serve or be served, it does tend to cloy the palate as successive courses are produced. By the time the dessert is served, the champagne, instead of being a splendid finale to the meal, becomes merely dull. Champagne should be kept in its rightful place: quite simply, as the best of aperitif drinks.

The prudent attitude to non-sparkling white table wines can be summed up thus: they should be served only with so-called white meat (chicken, veal and young lamb) and they should be as dry as possible. The cheaper white wines should be served refrigerator-cold; the better ones, Burgundy for instance, should be just chilled. Any white wine which is even slightly sweet should be kept strictly away from red meat. It is true that some Frenchmen are known to serve vintage Sauternes with their foie gras, but it's an eccentric taste at best.

SERVING WINE

White wine should be refrigerated or chilled uncorked and opened just before pouring. If the wine is red, draw the cork at least an hour before you are ready to pour it, or decant it if you prefer. The important thing is to allow the air to reach the wine. This applies to any red wine you have chosen, whether it is from Argentina or Andalusia. The difference that one hour will make to the taste of the wine is remarkable, and is evidence that you care about what your guests are to drink.

Anthony Hern

SAUCES, STUFFINGS AND GARNISHES

There are certain accompaniments which are traditionally served with meat, such as Yorkshire pudding with roast beef - it would be hard to think of one without the other. There are many others: mustard and horseradish with beef, mint sauce with lamb, apple sauce with pork, bread sauce with chicken and cranberry sauce with turkey, but there are plenty of other flavours with which to enhance your cooking. For instance, try apricot with roast lamb, pineapple with gammon or baked apples with pork. Never be afraid to experiment with accompaniments, for they put the individual signature on a dish.

Sauces

The most important thing to remember about sauces is that they should be well flavoured. Be generous with the mint in mint sauce and try making your own cranberry sauce for a change. Leave apple sauce chunky or purée it, according to your own preference. Sauces are made to different consistencies, depending on whether they are to be used for coating the ingredients while cooking or to be poured over a dish after it is cooked. Vinaigrette is delicious with all cold meats, but make it more interesting by adding chopped parsley, onion and garlic to the basic oil and vinegar (or lemon juice) dressing.

Stuffings

Stuffing is particularly useful with poultry for, not only does it help maintain the shape of the bird and keep the flesh moist during cooking, but it is also useful in helping to make all meat go further. Apart from these practical considerations, stuffing is simply good to eat. Its flavour is absorbed by the meat during cooking and it adds enormously to the interest of the dish.

Choose stuffing ingredients that both complement and contrast with the flavour of the meat. Sage and onion is an old favourite with duck and goose, but a fruity flavour such as apple, apricot, prune or cherry goes rather well with these fatty birds.

If you use one of the excellent packets of stuffing mix available everywhere, do add something of your own to it. Thyme and parsley stuffing is used with chicken, beef, lamb and veal, but add chopped onion or bacon, ham, grated lemon or orange peel to make it more interesting. Celery and onion or chestnut and apple are delicious with turkey. If you are planning to stuff a turkey with sausagemeat, make it less bland by adding garlic, onion, apple, celery or capers first.

To check the seasoning of a stuffing, you should fry a small ball of the mixture before the bird is stuffed. Taste the ball of stuffing and adjust the seasoning accordingly.

Garnishes

A dish is made to look colourful and attractive by the addition of garnishes. These add the finishing touch to any dish and allow plenty of scope for ingenuity. Croûtons, watercress and orange twists or lemon wedges are all good garnishes for various meat dishes, but herbs of all kinds are particularly useful. I keep a bunch of parsley and sprigs of chervil and dill in a mug in a cool part of the kitchen and use them to add to the visual attraction of meat dishes. If you want herbs to stay fresh longer, wash them and put in a polythene bag in the refrigerator.

CRANBERRY SAUCE

6 oz (175g) castor sugar
¼ pt (150ml) water
8 oz (225g) fresh cranberries

Put the sugar in a small saucepan with the water and stir over low heat until the sugar has dissolved. Meanwhile wash the cranberries and remove any stalks. Add to the sugar syrup and bring to the boil slowly. Simmer gently for about 10 minutes or until the berries are tender, stirring occasionally. Remove from the heat, turn into a small serving dish and serve warm.

Serve with roast turkey, pheasant or goose, or with roast pork.

Serves about 6.

TOMATO SAUCE

1 tbsp oil
1 streaky bacon rasher, chopped
1 large onion, chopped
1 oz (25g) plain flour
14 oz (397g) can of peeled tomatoes or 12 oz (350g) ripe tomatoes, skinned and chopped
¼ pt (150ml) water
1 chicken Oxo cube
1 level tsp salt
Black pepper
1 tbsp Worcestershire sauce
1 level tsp sugar
1 bayleaf
1 clove of garlic, crushed

Cooking time: 25 minutes.

Heat the oil in a small saucepan and fry the bacon and onion for 5 minutes. Stir in the flour and cook for 1 minute. Add the tomatoes, water and crumbled Oxo cube and bring to the boil, stirring until thickened. Add the remaining ingredients, cover with a tight-fitting lid and simmer gently for 25 minutes, stirring occasionally.

Remove from the heat and sieve the sauce into a bowl. Rinse out the saucepan and return the sauce to it. Reheat the sauce. Taste and check seasoning.

This is a good sauce to serve with simple meat dishes.

RICH ONION SAUCE

2 oz (50g) dripping
8 oz (225g) onions, sliced
2 oz (50g) plain flour
1 pt (600ml) water
1 or 2 red Oxo cubes
3 tbsp tomato ketchup
A few drops of Worcestershire sauce
¼ level tsp dried marjoram
Salt and pepper

Cooking time: About 20 minutes.

Melt the dripping in a saucepan, add the onions and fry for 5-10 minutes or until golden brown. Stir in the flour and cook for 2 minutes. Add the water and the crumbled Oxo cube and bring to the boil, stirring until the sauce has thickened. Add the tomato ketchup, Worcestershire sauce, marjoram, salt and pepper and stir well. Cover with a lid, reduce the heat and simmer very gently for 20 minutes.

Serve with fried liver, meatballs, meat loaf or beefburgers.

PROVENÇALE SAUCE

2 tbsp oil
1 large onion, chopped
1 clove of garlic, crushed
14 oz (397g) can of peeled tomatoes
Salt and pepper
2 tbsp vinegar
2 level tsp sugar
2 tbsp soy sauce

Heat the oil in a small saucepan. Add the onion and garlic and fry for about 10 minutes or until the onion is soft and transparent. Add the tomatoes, salt and pepper and continue cooking for a further 15 minutes or until the tomatoes have been reduced to a thick purée. Stir in the vinegar, sugar and soy sauce and cook for a further 1-2 minutes. Taste and check seasoning. Turn into a small serving bowl and serve hot.

Serve with fondue bourguignonne, sausages or chops.

MINT SAUCE

A bunch of mint (about 8 large sprigs)
2 level tsp castor sugar
1 tbsp boiling water
2 tbsp vinegar

Wash and dry the mint well, then strip the leaves from the stems and chop very finely. Place the sugar in a sauce boat with the boiling water and stir until the sugar has dissolved. Add the chopped mint and vinegar to taste. Add a little extra sugar if necessary.

This makes just under ¼ pt (150ml) mint sauce. Serve with roast lamb or grilled lamb chops.

Cranberry Sauce

Rich Onion Sauce

Tomato Sauce

Cumberland Sauce

Mint Sauce

Horseradish Sauce

Provençale Sauce

Apple Sauce

Sage and Onion Stuffing

Yorkshire Pudding

Tartar Sauce

B⁻ead Sauce

Curried Mayonnaise

Parsley and Thyme Stuffing

Special Kebab Rice

Pease Pudding

APPLE SAUCE

1 lb (450g) cooking apples
5 tbsp water
Juice of half a lemon
1 oz (25g) butter
Sugar (to taste)

Peel, core and slice the apples. Place them in a saucepan with the water and lemon juice. Cover and cook gently until the apples are soft, stirring occasionally. Beat well with a wooden spoon until smooth. Add the butter and sugar to taste.

Serve with duck, goose or pork.

CUMBERLAND SAUCE

2 oranges
2 lemons
8 oz (225g) redcurrant jelly
1 wineglass of red wine or port
About 2 heaped tsp arrowroot
2 tbsp cold water

Using a vegetable peeler, peel the rind from the oranges and lemons. Cut the fruit in half and squeeze out the juice. Strain the juice into a small saucepan, add the redcurrant jelly and stir over low heat until the jelly has melted and blended with the fruit juice.

Meanwhile shred the peel and place in a small saucepan, cover with cold water and bring to the boil. Strain and discard the water. Cover with fresh water and simmer for 20 minutes or until the peel is tender, then drain thoroughly.

Add the red wine or port to the jelly and bring to the boil, stirring constantly. Simmer for 2-3 minutes, then strain into a measuring jug.

For each ½ pt (300ml) of sauce, blend 1 heaped tsp of arrowroot with 1 tbsp of cold water in a cup. Stir into the sauce in the measuring jug. Replace in the saucepan and bring to the boil, stirring constantly until the sauce has thickened. Stir in the peel and pour into a dish. Any remaining sauce may be stored in small jars and kept in a very cool place.

Serve with cold ham or gammon.

HORSERADISH SAUCE

¼ pt (150ml) double cream
2 level tbsp grated horseradish
1 tsp cider or wine vinegar
Salt and black pepper
A little castor sugar

Lightly whip the cream and add the horseradish. Stir in the vinegar, salt and freshly ground pepper. Add a little sugar to taste and blend thoroughly. Turn into a small serving pot, cover with foil or cling film and chill well before serving.

Serve this sauce with a fondue or with roast beef or grilled steaks.

CURRIED MAYONNAISE

¼ pt (150ml) mayonnaise
1 tbsp lemon juice
1 level tsp curry powder
1 tbsp finely chopped mango chutney
Salt and black pepper

Mix together all the ingredients in a bowl. Turn into a small serving dish and serve.

Serve this sauce with a fondue or as a dip for sausages.

BREAD SAUCE

1 onion, peeled
2 cloves
1 pt (600ml) milk
3 oz (75g) white breadcrumbs
Salt and pepper
A knob of butter

Stick the cloves into the onion, then place in a saucepan with the milk. Bring to the boil very gently, then turn off the heat and leave the milk to infuse for 30 minutes.

Lift out the onion and stir in the breadcrumbs, salt, pepper and butter. Reheat the sauce almost to boiling point, then remove from the heat. Cover with a piece of damp greaseproof paper and keep warm.

TARTAR SAUCE

½ pt (300ml) good mayonnaise
1 rounded tbsp chopped gherkins
1 rounded tbsp chopped capers
1 rounded tbsp chopped parsley

Put the mayonnaise in a bowl, add the remaining ingredients and mix well. Turn into a serving bowl and serve.

This sauce goes particularly well with fried brains (see page 186), or veal.

Serve with roast chicken, turkey or pheasant.

THIN GRAVY

A little sherry and redcurrant jelly can be added to thin gravy for game birds. Pour all the fat from the roasting tin, leaving only the pan sediment. Add ½ pt (300ml) of stock made with 1 red or chicken Oxo cube. Stir well and boil for 2-3 minutes to reduce slightly.

Season and serve hot with a roast.

THICK GRAVY

Pour off most of the fat from the roasting tin, leaving about 2 tbsp of the sediment. Stir in 1 level tbsp of plain flour and blend thoroughly with the fat. Stir constantly with a wooden spoon until starting to brown and thicken. Gradually blend in ½ pt (300ml) of stock made with 1 red or chicken Oxo cube, bring to the boil and cook for 2–3 minutes.

Season to taste, strain and serve hot with a roast.

APRICOT GRAVY

1 oz (25g) flour
Syrup from a 7½ oz (213g) can of apricots
About ½ pt (300ml) water
1 red Oxo cube

Strain off most of the fat from the roasting tin, leaving 2 tbsp of the sediment. Stir in the flour and cook for 2-3 minutes. Add sufficient water to the apricot syrup to make it up to ¾ pt (450ml). Stir into the roasting tin with the crumbled Oxo cube and bring to the boil, stirring until thickened. Simmer for 3-4 minutes. Taste and check seasoning.

Serve with apricot stuffed lamb (see page 119).

ONION GRAVY

1 medium onion, chopped
¾ pt (450ml) water
½ level tsp salt
1 level tbsp cornflour
1 red Oxo cube

Place the onion and ¼ pt (150ml) of the water in a saucepan with the salt and bring to the boil. Cover with a lid and simmer for 15 minutes until tender. Blend the cornflour and the crumbled Oxo cube with the remaining water and stir into the onion mixture in the saucepan. Bring to the boil, stirring until thickened, and simmer for 1 minute. Taste and check seasoning.

This simple gravy is ideal to serve with joints, chops and sausages. It is also perfect for serving with liver dumplings (see page 185).

SAGE AND ONION STUFFING

1 lb (450g) onions, roughly chopped
½ pt (300ml) water
1 oz (25g) butter
1 level tsp dried sage
8 oz (225g) fresh white breadcrumbs
1 level tsp salt
Black pepper

Place the onions and water in a saucepan and bring to the boil. Simmer for 15 minutes, then drain well. Stir in the remaining ingredients and mix well.

Use as a stuffing for goose or pork. If you prefer to serve the stuffing separately, place in a greased heatproof dish and dot with butter, then cook in the oven with the bird for about 25 minutes or until the top is golden brown and crisp.

CHESTNUT AND WALNUT STUFFING

12 oz (350g) dried chestnuts (soaked overnight in hot water)
4 oz (100g) walnuts, chopped
8 oz (225g) streaky bacon, chopped
3 oz (75g) butter
4 oz (100g) brown breadcrumbs
1 egg, beaten
4 tbsp fresh, chopped parsley
1 tbsp castor sugar
2 level tsp salt
Freshly ground black pepper

Boil the chestnuts in water until just tender, then chop coarsely. Put in a bowl with the walnuts. Place the bacon in a saucepan and fry until the fat has run out. Add the nuts and fry gently to brown. Add the butter, allow to melt, then add the breadcrumbs and fry until brown. Turn into a bowl, add the remaining ingredients and mix very thoroughly.

This is sufficient to stuff a 15 lb (6.7kg) turkey.

PARSLEY AND THYME STUFFING

2 oz (50g) shredded suet
4 oz (100g) fresh white breadcrumbs
2 level tbsp chopped parsley
½ level tsp dried thyme
Rind of 1 lemon, finely grated
Salt and pepper
1 egg, beaten

Mix together the suet and breadcrumbs in a bowl. Add the parsley, thyme, lemon rind and plenty of salt and pepper. Mix together lightly with a fork. Stir in sufficient beaten egg to bind the stuffing together.

Use for stuffing veal, chicken or turkey. If you prefer to serve the stuffing separately, it may be shaped into small balls and used as savoury forcemeat balls.

PEASE PUDDING

The split peas used in this recipe may be yellow or green, though I find that most shops sell the yellow ones.

Traditionally, the peas were cooked in a pudding cloth in a pan with boiling pork or bacon, but in this recipe, which is to serve with faggots, the peas are cooked on their own.

8 oz (225g) split peas, soaked overnight in cold water
½ oz (12½g) dripping or butter
1 level tsp salt
Black pepper

Cooking time: About 2 hours.

Drain off the water from the peas. Place them in a saucepan with fresh water to cover. Cover with a lid and simmer gently for about 1 hour or until the peas are tender. Drain off any excess water. Put the peas in a bowl and mash very well with a fork or potato masher. Add the dripping or butter with the salt and plenty of freshly ground pepper. Turn into a greased 1 pt (600ml) pudding basin, cover with foil and steam for 1 hour. Turn into a warm serving dish.

If preferred, the mixture may be placed in a greased heatproof casserole and baked in the oven for about 30 minutes at 350°F (180°C) mark 4.

Serves 4.

ROAST POTATOES

1½ lb (675g) medium-sized old potatoes
Oil

Heat the oven to 425°F (220°C) mark 7.

Peel the potatoes and, if necessary, cut into even-sized pieces. Parboil in water for 3 minutes, then drain well.

Pour the oil into a suitable sized roasting tin to a depth of ¼ in. (0.6cm) – or use dripping, which gives a good flavour but doesn't crisp the potatoes so well. Place the tin near the top of the oven until the oil or fat is sizzling. Add the potatoes and roast, turning occasionally, for about 1¼ hours or until the potatoes are crisp and golden brown.

Serve with roasts of all kinds: beef, lamb, pork, chicken, turkey, duck, goose and veal.

Serves 4.

SPECIAL KEBAB RICE

1 oz (25g) butter
1 tbsp oil
1 large onion, finely chopped
6 oz (175g) easy-cook rice
½ pt (300ml) water
1 level tsp salt
Black pepper

Cooking time: About 15 minutes.

Melt the butter and oil together in a pan, add the onion and cover with a lid. Simmer for about 5 minutes or until the onion is softened but not coloured. Add the rice, water and freshly ground pepper, salt, and bring

to the boil. Reduce the heat and cover with a lid. Simmer for about 10 minutes or until all the water has been absorbed, then stir. Taste and check seasoning.

This savoury onion rice is especially good with kebabs, and can be cooked while the kebabs are grilling.

Serves 4.

YORKSHIRE PUDDING

4 oz (100g) plain flour
¼ level tsp salt
1 egg, beaten
½ pt (300ml) milk and water, mixed
A little fat or dripping

Cooking time: About 15 or 30 minutes, depending on size.

Heat the oven to 425°F (220°C) mark 7.

Sift the flour and salt into a bowl. Make a well in the centre of the flour and blend in the egg with a little of the milk and water, using a small wire whisk to make a smooth paste. Blend in the remaining milk and water to make a batter (the mixture will be the consistency of pouring cream). Beat really well.

Place a little fat or dripping in the bottom of a shallow Yorkshire pudding tin or in the base of a 12-hole deep patty tin and heat in the oven until the fat has melted and is very hot. Remove the tin from the oven and pour in the batter. Return to the oven and cook the large Yorkshire pudding for about 30 minutes or until well risen, crisp and golden brown, or for about 15 minutes if making the small puddings. Serve at once.

Serve with roast beef.

Serves 4-6.

BEEF
RECIPES

Boned and rolled sirloin — a classic beef roast (see pages 12-13 for roasting instructions). Serve with the traditional accompaniments of Yorkshire puddings, roast potatoes and gravy (see pages 55-60).

GARDENER'S BEEF

This dish is a meal in itself, and is particularly satisfying if you use vegetables that you have grown yourself in the garden.

1 oz (25g) dripping
1½ lb (675g) stewing steak
1 oz (25g) plain flour
1 pt (600ml) water
2 red Oxo cubes
1½ level tsp salt
Black pepper
1 bayleaf
1 large leek, sliced
2 carrots, peeled and quartered
1 parsnip, peeled and diced
1 turnip, peeled and diced
4 potatoes, peeled and quartered

Cooking time: About 3 hours.

Heat the oven to 325°F (160°C) mark 3.

Cut the meat into 1 in. (2.5cm) cubes. Melt the dripping in a frying pan and quickly fry the meat to seal the juices and brown. Stir in the flour and cook for 2 minutes until lightly browned. Blend in the water and the crumbled Oxo cubes and bring to the boil, stirring until the sauce has thickened. Add the salt, freshly ground pepper and bayleaf and turn into a large 4 pt (2.3l) heatproof casserole. Cover with a lid or foil and cook in the oven for 1½ hours.

Add the vegetables to the casserole, return to the oven and continue cooking for a further 1½ hours or until the vegetables and meat are tender. Taste and check seasoning. Remove the bayleaf.

Serves 4-6.

Top: Gardener's Beef.
Bottom: Steak and Kidney Pie.

STEAK AND KIDNEY PIE

The best cut of beef to use in steak and kidney pie is skirt, which is sometimes difficult to get as there is only a limited amount on each side of beef. You should therefore order it from your butcher in advance. It is usually the same price as other stewing beef. Beef kidney is best: buy it in one large piece, then remove the white suet part yourself and cut it into pieces. Do not buy ready-mixed steak and kidney as it is not such good value.

1 lb (450g) skirt beef
8 oz (225g) beef kidney
1 oz (25g) plain flour
1 oz (25g) dripping
1 large onion, chopped
½ pt (300ml) water
1 red Oxo cube
1 level tsp salt
Black pepper
4 oz (100g) mushrooms, sliced
7½ oz (212g) packet of puff pastry, thawed

Cooking time: About 2½ hours.

Cut the steak and kidney into 1 in. (2.5cm) cubes, put them in a polythene bag with the flour and toss until well coated. Melt the dripping in a saucepan, add the meat and onion and fry until browned. Stir in the water and crumbled Oxo cube and bring to the boil, stirring constantly. Season with salt and freshly ground pepper. Partially cover the pan and simmer for 1½ hours or until the meat is almost tender. Stir in the mushrooms and continue cooking for a further 30 minutes or until the meat is really tender. Taste and check seasoning. Turn into a 1½ pt (900ml) pie dish and allow to become quite cold. Place a pie funnel in the centre.

Heat the oven to 425°F (220°C) mark 7.

Roll out the pastry on a lightly floured surface and cover the pie with it. Seal and crimp the edges, make a small slit in the centre to allow the steam to escape and use any pastry trimmings to decorate the top of the pie. Brush with milk and cook in the oven for 30-35 minutes or until the pastry is well risen and golden brown and the meat is hot through. If the pastry is getting too brown, cover with foil.

Accompaniments: Serve with boiled potatoes and carrots.

Serves 6.

FRUGAL MEAT LOAF

A low budget meat loaf, which needs a good sauce, such as rich onion or tomato, to accompany it (see page 55).

12 oz (350g) minced beef
8 oz (225g) beef sausagemeat
2½ oz (62g) fresh white breadcrumbs
1 level tbsp fresh, chopped mixed herbs
1 small onion, grated
1 red Oxo cube, crumbled
1 egg
Salt and pepper

Cooking time: 1¼-1½ hours.

Heat the oven to 350°F (180°C) mark 4.

Put all the ingredients in a bowl and mix together very thoroughly. Press firmly into a 1 lb (450g) loaf tin and pack down well. Cook in the oven for 1¼-1½ hours. Drain off any fat and turn the loaf onto a warm serving dish. Serve with a sauce.

Accompaniments: Sliced carrots and creamy mashed potatoes go very well with this meat loaf.

Serves 6.

SCOTCH MINCE

My mother is a Scot and she taught me how to make this very simple recipe. The porridge oats make the mince go further and thicken it too. Try adding oats to a casserole if you want it to go further or if you want it to be a little thicker in consistency. This dish is a great favourite with children.

A knob of dripping
1 lb (450g) lean minced beef
1 small onion, chopped
1 oz (25g) porridge oats
1 red Oxo cube
¾ pt (450ml) water
Salt and black pepper

Cooking time: About 1 hour.

Melt the dripping in a saucepan over low heat, add the minced beef and fry gently to allow the fat to run out. Increase the heat and fry until brown. Add the onion and oats, stir in the crumbled Oxo cube and water and bring to the boil, stirring constantly. Season with salt and freshly ground pepper. Cover with a lid or foil and simmer for 1 hour or until the beef is tender.

Alternatively, the mince may be turned into a heatproof casserole and cooked in the oven at 350°F (180°C) mark 4 for 1 hour.

Accompaniments: Serve with boiled or mashed potatoes and either carrots or a green vegetable such as buttered cabbage or Brussels sprouts.

Serves 4.

Top: Frugal Meat Loaf.
Bottom: Scotch Mince.

SWISS FONDUE

Having a fondue party is a fun idea. Not only do you enjoy yourself, but your friends are kept busy cooking their own supper. Once they master the idea, they will enjoy dabbling in the various sauces. For fondue bourguignonne, cubes of tender steak are fried in oil on skewers and served with a selection of sauces and salads. There is no need for potatoes – simply serve crisp French bread with plenty of butter and a green salad.

6-8 oz (175-225g) rump steak per person or
6-8 oz (175-225g) leg fillet of lamb per person or
8 oz (225g) pork cocktail sausages per person

Sufficient vegetable oil for frying to fill the fondue pot one-third full

Cut the beef or lamb into ½ in. (1.25cm) cubes. Heat the oil on the hob of the cooker in the kitchen until a faint haze is rising, then place it on the fondue stove. Remember that the oil will heat more quickly with a lid on the pan, but watch it carefully as it should not become too hot. On no account should you leave it unattended.

Mark the skewers with coloured tapes or wools so that each guest will know which is his. If using metal skewers or forks, be sure to let them cool before anybody puts one into his mouth. It is better still to transfer the meat onto ordinary table forks of different patterns.

Keep the oil hot by returning it to the cooker at intervals and not cooking more than 6 portions at the same time. Your guests can time their own steak cubes as some will like them rarer than others.

Accompaniments: A selection of sauces to dip the meat into (see pages 55 – 60) with French bread and a green salad. A warming hot punch – Glühwein as this is called in Switzerland and Austria – is a perfect accompaniment. Lace it with cheap brandy if you have some to hand.

Serves 6.

Left: Swiss Fondue.
Right: Alpine Steak.

ALPINE STEAK

This is a good meaty casserole which is perfect on a cold winter's evening.

4 slices topside of beef (each about 6 oz [175g] in weight)
1½ oz (40g) plain flour
1 level tsp salt
¼ level tsp pepper
1½ oz (40g) lard or dripping
2 large onions, finely sliced
2 sticks of celery, sliced
8 oz (227g) can of peeled tomatoes
2 level tsp tomato purée
1 tsp Worcestershire sauce
¼ pt (150ml) water
1 red Oxo cube

Cooking time: About 2½ hours.

Heat the oven to 300°F (150°C) mark 2.

Cut the beef into 8 pieces. Mix together the flour, salt and pepper and toss the meat in this mixture, pressing it so that most of the flour is used. Melt the lard or dripping in a frying pan and fry the meat quickly on all sides until browned. Lift it out and place in a heatproof casserole.

Add the onions and celery to the fat remaining in the pan and fry until pale golden brown, then add to the meat in the casserole. If there is any flour left over, stir it into the vegetables and cook for 1 minute. Add the tomatoes, tomato purée, Worcestershire sauce, water and crumbled Oxo cube to the casserole. Cover with a lid or foil and cook in the oven for about 2½ hours or until the meat is tender.

Accompaniments: I like this dish served with boiled potatoes and a green vegetable such as Brussels sprouts or broccoli.

Serves 4.

CARBONNADE OF BEEF

Use stewing steak, such as shin or skirt, for this recipe and cook it slowly to allow the flavour of the ale to enhance the sauce.

1½ lb (675g) stewing steak
1½ oz (40g) dripping
8 oz (225g) onions, sliced
2 large carrots, sliced
1½ oz (40g) plain flour
¾ pt (450ml) pale or brown ale
1½ level tsp salt
1 rounded tbsp demerara sugar
1½ level tsp made mustard
Black pepper

Cooking time: About 3-4 hours.

Cut the meat into strips ½ in. (1.25cm) thick. Melt the dripping in a saucepan, add the meat and brown quickly. Lift it out with a slotted spoon and keep on one side. Add the onions and carrots to the pan and fry until golden brown. Stir in the flour and cook for 1 minute. Blend in the pale or brown ale and bring to the boil, stirring until thickened. Add the remaining ingredients and the meat to the pan. Stir until blended, cover with a lid or foil and simmer very gently for 3-4 hours or until the meat is tender. Taste and check seasoning. Turn into a warm serving dish.

Accompaniments: Serve with braised celery or parsnips, and creamy mashed potatoes to soak up the gravy.

Serves 4-6.

Top: Carbonnade of Beef.
Bottom: Belgian Pot Roast.

BELGIAN POT ROAST

Pot roasting is particularly suitable for those small, slightly tougher joints of beef such as brisket, silverside, and back and top ribs. The meat is quickly fried to brown all over, then cooked very slowly on a bed of vegetables until tender and cooked through. If preferred, the meat may be pot roasted in the oven. When it comes to the boil, remove from the hob and cook in the oven at 325°F (160°C) mark 3 for about 2 hours.

2 lb (900g) silverside of beef
Plain flour (to coat)
1 oz (25g) dripping
2 onions, quartered
3 carrots, sliced
2 parsnips, diced
3 sticks of celery, sliced
Salt and pepper
1 bayleaf
¼ pt (150ml) beer
½ oz (12½g) cornflour
2 tbsp cold water

Cooking time: About 2 hours.

Coat the meat in the flour. Melt the dripping in a large saucepan and quickly fry the meat to brown on all sides. Lift it out of the pan and keep on one side. Add all the vegetables to the pan and fry for 2-3 minutes. Season well with salt and pepper, add the bayleaf and arrange the meat on top. Pour over the beer to cover the vegetables (add more beer if necessary). Cover with a tight-fitting lid and simmer very gently for about 30 minutes to the lb (450g) plus an extra 30 minutes.

Lift out the meat and place on a warm serving dish. Strain the vegetables, remove the bayleaf and spoon the cooking liquor around the meat (there should be about ¾ pt [450ml] of this; if necessary, make it up with extra beer or water). Blend the cornflour with the cold water and add to the pan with the beer. Bring to the boil, stirring constantly until thickened. Taste and check seasoning. Serve in a sauce boat with the pot roast and vegetables.

Accompaniments: Serve with plain boiled potatoes.

Serves 6.

SPANISH BEEF OLIVES

This recipe can also be made with thinly beaten chicken breasts instead of beef, in which case the cooking time should be cut by about 30 minutes.

4 slices of silverside or topside of beef (weighing about 5 oz [150g] each)
4 oz (100g) butter
1 medium onion, chopped
4 oz (100g) mushrooms, chopped
1 oz (25g) stuffed green olives, chopped
2 oz (50g) fresh white breadcrumbs
1 egg, beaten
Salt and pepper
1 large orange
1 oz (25g) plain flour
¼ pt (150ml) water
1 red Oxo cube

Cooking time: About 1½ hours.

Trim off any fat from the meat. Place each slice in turn between wet greaseproof paper, then beat flat with a rolling pin. (Using wet paper prevents the meat from sticking to the rolling pin.)

To prepare the stuffing: Melt half of the butter in a saucepan and fry the onion for 5-8 minutes or until soft but not brown. Add the mushrooms and cook for a further 2 minutes. Remove the pan from the heat and stir in the olives, breadcrumbs, egg, salt and pepper and mix thoroughly.

Divide the stuffing into 4 equal parts and place a portion on each slice of meat. Roll up the meat and tie neatly with thin string or secure with wooden cocktail sticks. Peel thin strips of rind from the orange, then cut into thin matchsticks with a sharp knife. Cut some slices from the orange for garnish. Squeeze the juice from the orange, pour it into a measuring jug and make up to ½ pt (300ml) with water.

Melt the remaining butter in a saucepan and fry the beef olives to brown all over. Lift them out and keep on one side. Stir the flour into the fat remaining in the pan and cook for 2 minutes. Blend in the water and orange juice with the crumbled Oxo cube and bring to the boil, stirring constantly. Return the meat to the pan, cover with a lid or foil and simmer gently for about 1½ hours or until the beef is tender.

Lift out the beef olives and place on a serving dish. Remove the string or cocktail sticks. Taste sauce and check seasoning. Spoon the sauce over the meat, sprinkle with the strips of orange rind and garnish with slices of orange. Serve immediately.

Accompaniments: Serve with creamed potatoes and garden peas.

Serves 4.

CHILLI CON CARNE

For this recipe, use a well-known brand of chilli powder or seasoning, as some others can be too strong.

6 oz (175g) dried red kidney beans
2 tbsp oil
2 onions, chopped
2 cloves of garlic, crushed
1 large green pepper, seeded and roughly chopped
1 lb (450g) minced beef
14 oz (397g) can of peeled tomatoes
¼ pt (150ml) water
1 red Oxo cube
1-2 level tsp chilli powder or seasoning
1 level tsp paprika pepper
2 level tsp salt
Black pepper

Cooking time: About 1 hour 10 minutes.

Put the beans in a bowl, cover with cold water and leave to soak overnight.

The following day, drain the beans and boil in fresh water for at least 10 minutes. Heat the oil in a saucepan, add the

Top: Chilli con Carne.
Bottom: Spanish Beef Olives.

Chilli con Carne continued from page 70.

onions, garlic, green pepper and beef and fry for 5 minutes, stirring constantly. Add the tomatoes, water, crumbled Oxo cube, chilli powder or seasoning, paprika pepper, salt and freshly ground pepper and bring to the boil, stirring constantly. Drain the beans, add to the pan, stir well, then cover with a lid or foil and simmer for about 1 hour or until the beans are soft. Taste and check seasoning. Turn into a warm dish and serve.

If preferred, this dish may be made in advance and reheated in a hot oven (425°F [220°C] mark 7) for about 30 minutes or over moderate heat on the hob, stirring from time to time until piping hot.

Accompaniments: Serve with a large bowl of plain boiled rice and a tossed green salad.

Serves 4.

EASY ONION STEAK

This is a dish which is so easy to prepare, and is ideal to leave in the oven while you are out.

1.6 oz (46g) packet of thick onion soup mix
1½ lb (675g) chuck steak in one piece (about 1 in. [2.5cm] thick)
1 oz (25g) butter

Cooking time: About 3 hours.

Heat the oven to 300°F (150°C) mark 2.

Put a large piece of foil on a baking sheet or heatproof dish and sprinkle half of the soup mix onto it. Place the steak on top, and sprinkle over the remaining soup mix. Dot with small pieces of butter and loosely seal the foil. Cook undisturbed in the oven for about 3 hours. Serve either straight from the foil or lift it out onto a serving dish. Spoon any juices in the foil over the meat.

Accompaniments: Serve with a rich onion gravy or sauce (see pages 59 and 55) or, if preferred, a thin gravy. Jacket potatoes and braised celery or carrots cooked beside the beef in the oven will make this a complete oven meal.

Serves 4.

HOT SPICED BEEF WITH GINGER

Use a commercial brand of chilli powder in this recipe rather than one bought from an Indian shop. The Indian ones are very, very hot, while the commercial brands are blended with other spices and are much milder.

2 lb (900g) braising steak
2 onions, chopped
1 oz (25g) plain flour
1 level tsp salt
Black pepper
1 level tsp ground ginger
2 oz (50g) dripping

Sauce
½ tsp chilli powder
8 oz (227g) can of peeled tomatoes
1 tbsp Worcestershire sauce
1 oz (25g) soft brown sugar
2 tbsp wine vinegar
2 cloves of garlic, crushed
1 bayleaf
15 oz (425g) can of red kidney beans
¼ pt (150ml) soured cream

Cooking time: About 2 hours.

Heat the oven to 325°F (160°C) mark 3.

Cut the beef into 1 in. (2.5cm) cubes and chop the onions. Mix together the flour, salt, freshly ground pepper and ginger and use this to coat the meat.

Heat the dripping in a large saucepan, add the beef and onions and fry quickly to brown. Lift them out with a slotted spoon and place in a 3 pt (1.7l) heatproof casserole. In the pan, combine all the sauce ingredients except the beans and cream and pour over the meat. Cover with a lid or foil and cook in the oven for about 2 hours or until the beef is tender.

Remove the casserole from the oven, drain the can of beans and stir into the casserole. Return to the oven and cook for a further 15 minutes to heat through. Taste and check seasoning. Remove the bayleaf. When ready to serve, lightly stir in the cream to give an attractive swirled appearance on the top of the casserole.

Accompaniments: Serve with a tossed green salad and plain boiled rice.

Serves 6.

STEAK IN RED WINE

Use really small, white button mushrooms for this recipe and slice them finely.

4 pieces of rump steak (each about 6 oz [175g] in weight)
Oil
Black pepper
¼ pt (150ml) inexpensive red wine
4 oz (100g) small button mushrooms, sliced
2 oz (50g) butter
Salt

Cooking time: About 8 minutes.

An hour before cooking, oil the steaks and season well with freshly ground pepper.

Heat a thick frying pan and fry the steaks, without adding any extra fat, for 1 minute. Add the wine, reduce the heat and simmer for 4 minutes, turning once. Lift out the steaks and place on a warm serving dish. Add the mushrooms to the pan and cook quickly for 3 minutes. Add the butter and mix well so that it melts and blends with the wine. Taste and add the salt and a little more freshly ground pepper. Pour over the steaks and serve immediately.

Accompaniments: Serve with new potatoes and broccoli.

Serves 4.

STEAK DIANE

Use thin pieces of rump steak for this recipe.

6 oz (175g) unsalted butter
1 onion, finely chopped
4 pieces of rump steak (each about 6 oz [175g] in weight, and about ¼ in. [0.6cm] thick)
Grated rind and juice of 1 large lemon
A few drops of Worcestershire sauce
1 level tbsp fresh, chopped parsley
2 tbsp brandy

Cooking time: About 8 minutes.

Melt 2 oz (50g) of the butter in a large heavy frying pan, add the onion and fry for 5 minutes. Lift it out with a slotted spoon and keep warm.

Add the remaining butter to the pan and fry the steaks for 1 minute on each side over high heat. Lift them out, place on a serving dish and keep warm.

Return the onion to the pan. Stir in the lemon rind and juice and Worcestershire sauce. Add the parsley and brandy, ignite the brandy and pour over the steaks. Serve immediately.

Accompaniments: Serve with a green salad and new potatoes.

Serves 4.

BŒUF EN DAUBE

A daube is a French method of cooking meat, usually beef, and involves long, slow cooking in wine and stock. I find that this recipe is especially good if it's cooked the day before it is needed, then chilled in the refrigerator overnight. Any fat can be lifted off before reheating.

1½ lb (675g) stewing steak
4 oz (100g) piece of unsmoked, streaky bacon
½ pt (300ml) inexpensive red wine
4 tbsp oil
¾ lb (350g) carrots, sliced
¾ lb (350g) onions, sliced
1 clove of garlic, crushed
1 rounded tbsp tomato purée
¾ pt (450ml) water
1 red Oxo cube
1½ level tsp salt
Black pepper
1 bayleaf
1 sprig of parsley

Cooking time: About 3-4 hours.

Trim any excess fat from the meat and cut it into neat 1 in. (2.5cm) cubes. Trim off the rind and any bone from the bacon and cut the lean meat into strips. Put the meat and bacon in a large bowl and pour over the wine. Cover and leave in a cool place to marinate for several hours.

Heat the oven to 300°F (150°C) mark 2.

Heat the oil in a frying pan, lift the meat from the marinade and fry quickly to brown. Lift it out with a slotted spoon and put in a heatproof casserole about 4½ pt (2.5l) in capacity. Add the vegetables and garlic to the pan and fry for 2-3 minutes. Lift them out and add to the casserole with the meat. Add to the pan the marinade, tomato purée, water, crumbled Oxo cube, salt, freshly ground pepper, bayleaf and parsley and bring to the boil, stirring constantly. Pour into the casserole, cover with a lid or foil and cook in the oven for 3-4 hours or until the beef is tender. Taste and check seasoning. Remove the bayleaf and parsley.

Accompaniments: Serve with potatoes and peas.

Serves 4-6.

ROAST FILLET OF BEEF DIJONNAISE

For this dish, which includes a tasty Dijon mustard cream sauce, you should ask your butcher to cut the piece of meat from the thick end of the fillet. Ask him for a thin piece of fat the size of the fillet, too.

2 lb (900g) beef fillet
Salt and pepper
1 oz (25g) butter
1 level tbsp Dijon mustard
2 tbsp brandy
¼ pt (150ml) single cream
Sprigs of parsley (to garnish)

Heat the oven to 425°F (220°C) mark 7.

Trim away any sinews from the fillet and season well with salt and pepper. Cover the meat with the piece of fat and tie in place. Place the fillet in a roasting tin with the butter and roast in the oven according to taste. As a rough guide, allow 20 minutes for rare beef; 30 minutes for medium-rare beef; and 40 minutes for well-done beef.

Lift out the fillet and place on a warm serving dish. Remove the string. Remove the piece of fat, or leave it on top when serving if you prefer.

Skim off any fat in the roasting tin, add the mustard, brandy and cream and bring to the boil, stirring constantly. Boil for 1 minute, season with salt and pepper and pour over the meat. Garnish with sprigs of parsley. Serve immediately.

Accompaniments: Serve with jacket potatoes and a green salad, or with sauté potatoes, whole baked tomatoes and broccoli.

Serves 4.

Top: Bœuf en Daube.
Bottom: Roast Fillet of Beef Dijonnaise.

SPECIAL STEAK AND KIDNEY PUDDING

This recipe is for a traditional steak and kidney pudding such as might have been served in the nineteenth century. The suet crust pastry is richer than I use normally, but it works well. Use skirt beef if possible as it gives the best results.

1 lb (450g) skirt beef
12 oz (350g) ox kidney
1 medium onion, finely chopped
1 tbsp chopped parsley
4 oz (100g) mushrooms, sliced
1 level tsp salt
¼ level tsp pepper
A few drops of Worcestershire sauce
¼ pt (150ml) water
Suet crust pastry
8 oz (225g) self-raising flour
6 oz (175g) shredded suet
1 level tsp salt
About 9-10 tbsp cold water

Cooking time: About 3½-4 hours.

Grease a 2 pt (1l) pudding basin. Cut the steak and kidney into ½ in. (1.25cm) cubes, removing any fat. Use scissors to remove the core from the kidney. Put the steak and kidney in a bowl with the onion, parsley, mushrooms, salt, pepper and Worcestershire sauce and mix together well.

To make the pastry: Put the flour, suet and salt in a bowl and gradually add the water. Mix to a soft but not sticky dough. Take one-third of the pastry and roll out on a lightly floured surface to a circle large enough to cover the top of the basin. Roll out the remaining pastry and use it to line the basin.

Fill the basin with the meat mixture and add the water. Dampen the edges of the pastry and cover with the pastry lid. Press the pastry edges together firmly to seal. Cover the pudding with a piece of greased greaseproof paper with a pleat in it, then a lid of foil.

Stand the basin in a saucepan and pour boiling water into the pan until it comes halfway up the sides of the basin. Boil gently for 3½-4 hours, topping up with boiling water when necessary. When cooked, lift out the pudding and remove the greaseproof paper and foil. Stand the basin on a plate, wrap a napkin around it and serve the pudding immediately.

Accompaniments: Serve with boiled potatoes and carrots.

Serves 6.

OLD-FASHIONED SPICED BEEF

The beef will have to be ordered at least 10 days in advance from a good butcher who has a brine tub or vat, in order that the meat can be soaked in it for a week.

4 lb (1.8kg) piece of pickled salt silverside of beef, boned and rolled
1 level tsp ground ginger
1 level tsp nutmeg
1 level tsp ground black pepper
About 6 spring onions (to garnish)

Cooking time: About 3 hours.

Place the beef, ginger, nutmeg and pepper in a heavy saucepan and pour over sufficient cold water to cover. Cover with a lid and bring to the boil. Reduce the heat and simmer very gently for about 3 hours or until just tender.

Remove the pan from the heat and leave in a cool place until the stock and beef are quite cold. Lift out the meat and put on a plate. Cover with foil or cling film and chill in the refrigerator, preferably overnight.

Cut the beef in thin slices, garnish with the spring onions and serve with mustard.

Accompaniments: Serve with jacket potatoes and a selection of salads.

Serves at least 10 (or more, if served with other cold meats).

Top: Special Steak and Kidney Pudding.
Bottom: Old-fashioned Spiced Beef.

SAVOURY PANCAKES

For this recipe, use a pancake, omelette or frying pan, preferably of the non-stick variety. True pancake pans are very shallow so the pancakes can be turned easily. Unfilled pancakes keep in the refrigerator for three days or in the freezer for up to three months. If you want to keep the pancakes, make them, then spread them out to cool. If you have time, interleave them with greaseproof paper, then wrap them in foil. I have found that there is no need to put greaseproof paper between the pancakes if you thaw them completely before carefully prising them apart. They are then ready to be filled as detailed below.

Filling

2 streaky bacon rashers, chopped
1 lb (450g) minced beef
1 onion, chopped
1 stick of celery, chopped
1 level tbsp plain flour
¼ pt (150ml) water
1 red Oxo cube
2 level tbsp tomato purée
1 level tsp salt
Black pepper

Sauce

1 oz (25g) butter
1 oz (25g) plain flour
½ pt (300ml) milk
½ level tsp made English mustard
Salt and pepper
4 oz (100g) Cheddar cheese, grated

8 plain pancakes
1 sprig of parsley (to garnish)

Cooking time: About 20-30 minutes.

First prepare the filling: Place the bacon, beef, onion and celery in a saucepan and cook gently for 5-10 minutes to allow the fat to run out. Stir in the flour, crumble the Oxo cube in the water, add to the pan and bring to the boil, stirring constantly. Add all the remaining ingredients for the filling, cover with a lid or foil and simmer for 30-40 minutes or until tender.

Meanwhile make the sauce: Melt the butter in a small saucepan, stir in the flour and cook for 1 minute. Blend in the milk and bring to the boil, stirring until thickened. Simmer for 2 minutes. Add the mustard, salt, pepper and 3 oz (75g) of the cheese. Stir until the cheese has melted.

Spread the pancakes flat and divide the meat mixture between them. Roll them up, arrange in a single layer in a shallow heatproof dish and keep warm. Spoon over the cheese sauce and sprinkle with the remaining cheese. Cook under a moderate grill until the top is golden brown and bubbling. Garnish with the parsley and serve immediately.

If preferred, the pancakes may be stacked. Place a pancake in the bottom of a deep, round, heatproof dish. Cover with a thin layer of meat filling. Repeat until all the pancakes and filling have been used, finishing with a pancake. Pour over the cheese sauce, sprinkle with the remaining cheese and cook in a moderate oven (375°F [190°C] mark 5) for about 30 minutes or until hot through and golden brown and bubbling.

If you have made the pancakes in advance, reheat them in the oven at 375°F (190°C) mark 5 for 20-30 minutes.

Accompaniments: Serve the stuffed pancakes with a green salad and crispy French bread.

Serves 4.

Savoury Pancakes.

AMERICAN SAVOURY MINCE

This recipe was given to me by an American friend who served it for a crowd at a buffet lunch. It is ideal for this type of party as it is a recipe that is best made in advance and then reheated when required. It can be made the day before it is needed and left overnight in the refrigerator.

1 lb (450g) minced beef
3 large onions, chopped
1 large green pepper, seeded and sliced
3 sticks of celery, sliced
14 oz (397g) can of peeled tomatoes
½ pt (300ml) water
2 red Oxo cubes
3 tbsp tomato purée
Salt and pepper
8 oz (225g) quick-cook macaroni

Cooking time: About 45 minutes.

Place the minced beef and onions in a large saucepan and fry gently for 5 minutes to allow any fat to run out of the meat. Add the green pepper, celery, tomatoes, water and crumbled Oxo cubes and bring to the boil, stirring constantly. Add the tomato purée and plenty of salt and pepper. Cover with a lid, reduce the heat and simmer for 30 minutes.

Meanwhile cook the macaroni as directed on the packet, then drain well and stir into the meat mixture. Taste and check seasoning. Turn into a deep heatproof dish (about 4 pt [2.3l] capacity). Leave in a cool place until required.

To reheat: Cover with foil and cook in the oven at 375°F (190°C) mark 4 for about 45 minutes or until piping hot all through.

Accompaniments: This dish is almost a meal in itself, but is nice if served with a mixed green salad or a hot vegetable such as peas or beans.

Serves 6-8.

GREAT AMERICAN BEEFBURGERS

Home-made beefburgers are not always cheaper to buy than bought ones, but they do contain a larger proportion of meat. Take care not to overcook them otherwise they will shrink and become dry. They should be moist inside with a crispy brown outer coating.

1 lb (450g) good quality minced beef
8 oz (225g) beef sausagemeat
1 onion, grated
1 level tsp salt
Black pepper
A little flour
Dripping (to fry)

Cooking time: About 6 minutes.

Put the mince, sausagemeat, onion, salt and freshly ground pepper in a bowl and blend together well. Divide the mixture into 8 equal pieces and, on a lightly floured table and with floured hands, shape into beefburgers about 3 in. (7.5cm) in diameter.

Melt a little dripping in a frying pan and fry the beefburgers for about 3 minutes on each side or until cooked through. Lift them out and drain on kitchen paper. Arrange on a serving dish and serve immediately.

Accompaniments: Serve with vegetables and a tomato sauce (see page 55), or put into warm baps split in half and serve with fried onion rings.

Serves 4 or 8.

Top: American Savoury Mince.
Bottom: Great American Beefburgers.

COTTAGE PIE

This is one of those useful recipes that can be prepared in advance and then reheated when required. You could make the pie in small, individual portions if you prefer.

1 large onion, chopped
2 sticks of celery, sliced
1½ lb (675g) minced beef
1½ oz (40g) plain flour
2 red Oxo cubes
¼ pt (150ml) water
8 oz (227g) can of peeled tomatoes
Salt and pepper
2 lb (900g) potatoes
A little milk and butter
Sprigs of parsley (to garnish)

Cooking time: About 1 hour 25 minutes.

Place the onion, celery and minced beef in a large saucepan and cook gently for about 5 minutes to allow the fat to run out. Stir in the flour, add the crumbled Oxo cubes, water and tomatoes and bring to the boil, stirring constantly. Season well with salt and pepper. Reduce the heat, partially cover the pan with a lid and cook gently for about 45 minutes, stirring occasionally, until tender.

Meanwhile peel the potatoes and cook in boiling, salted water for about 15 minutes or until tender. Drain and mash well with milk and a knob of butter.

Place the meat in a heatproof dish, allow to cool slightly, then cover with the mashed potato.

When required, dot the potato with knobs of butter and reheat in the oven at 400°F (200°C) mark 6 for about 30 minutes or until the top is golden brown and the meat is hot through. Garnish with sprigs of parsley.

Accompaniments: A simple vegetable such as frozen peas can be cooked while the pie is in the oven.

Serves 6.

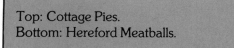

Top: Cottage Pies.
Bottom: Hereford Meatballs.

HEREFORD MEATBALLS

Simply use good minced beef mixed with some packet stuffing for these meatballs and then cook them in a piquant onion sauce for an easily prepared meal.

1 lb (450g) minced beef
1 oz (25g) lemon, parsley and thyme stuffing mix
1 egg, beaten
1 tsp salt
Black pepper
Sauce
1½ oz (40g) dripping
8 oz (225g) onions, chopped
1½ oz (40g) plain flour
¾ pt (450ml) water
1 red Oxo cube
3 tbsp tomato ketchup
Fresh, chopped parsley (to garnish)

Cooking time: About 45 minutes.

Put all the meatball ingredients in a bowl and mix together thoroughly. Divide the mixture into 12 equal pieces and, with lightly floured hands, shape into balls. Melt the dripping in a saucepan and quickly fry the meatballs until brown all over. Lift them out with a slotted spoon and put on a plate.

Add the onions to the dripping remaining in the pan and fry quickly to brown. Stir in the flour and cook for 2-3 minutes until beginning to brown. Blend in the water and crumbled Oxo cube and bring to the boil, stirring until thickened. Add the ketchup and season with salt and pepper to taste. Return the meatballs to the pan, cover with a lid, reduce the heat and simmer gently for about 45 minutes or until tender. Taste and check seasoning. Turn into a serving dish and sprinkle with parsley.

Accompaniments: Serve with any type of short-cut pasta, such as shells, macaroni or noodles, which are buttered and scattered with freshly chopped parsley, and a vegetable such as finely sliced carrots.

Serves 4.

CORNISH PASTIES

These pasties are delicious, easy to make and ideal for taking on a picnic. Use good quality meat, and take care to cut or shred it into tiny pieces so that it will be fully cooked.

Shortcrust pastry

8 oz (225g) plain flour
2 oz (50g) margarine
2 oz (50g) lard
About 3 tbsp cold water

Filling

8 oz (225g) lean chuck steak
1 medium potato
1 medium onion
½ level tsp dried mixed herbs
1 level tbsp chopped parsley
½ level tsp salt
Black pepper
2 tbsp stock or water (optional)

Cooking time: 45 minutes.

Put the flour in a bowl, cut the margarine and lard into small pieces and rub into the flour with the fingertips until the mixture resembles fine breadcrumbs. Add sufficient cold water to mix to a firm dough. Wrap in foil and chill in the refrigerator whilst making the filling.

Trim any fat from the meat, cut or shred the lean meat into small pieces and put in a bowl (this will take a little time but is well worth the trouble). Peel and finely dice the potato and finely chop the onion. Put these in the bowl with the meat and add the herbs, salt and freshly ground pepper. Add the water to make a moister mixture, if preferred.

Heat the oven to 400°F (200°C) mark 6.

Divide the pastry into 4 equal pieces and roll out each piece on a floured surface to a circle measuring 7 in. (17.5cm) in diameter. Trim the pastry, using a saucer or small plate to get a perfect shape.

Divide the filling into 4 equal parts, and place a portion in the centre of each pastry circle. Dampen the edges of the pastry, then draw them together firmly over the filling. Seal securely and crimp the edges neatly. Place on a baking sheet and brush with a little milk to glaze. Cook in the oven for 45 minutes or until the pastry is golden brown and the meat is tender.

Accompaniments: If it is a cold day, serve the pasties with a thick gravy (see page 59), and vegetables such as carrots or cabbage and braised celery. In summer serve with a mixed salad.

Serves 4.

MIDWEEK MEAT LOAF

Adding carrot to the meat loaf gives it an attractive appearance and a lovely flavour.

1 lb (450g) minced beef
3 oz (75g) fresh brown or white breadcrumbs
1 onion, finely grated
1 large carrot, finely grated
1 egg
1 level tsp salt
Black pepper
½ level tsp dried mixed herbs

Cooking time: About 1¼ hours.

Heat the oven to 350°F (180°C) mark 4.

Blend together all the ingredients in a bowl. Press firmly into a 1 lb (450g) loaf tin and smooth the top. Cook in the oven for about 1¼ hours or until the meat loaf has shrunk slightly from the sides of the tin and clear juices run out when a skewer is inserted in the middle of the loaf. Turn onto a warm serving dish and serve hot with gravy, or allow to become quite cold, then chill overnight in the refrigerator and serve sliced with salads.

Accompaniments: Serve this meat loaf with rich onion gravy or tomato sauce (see pages 59 and 55), creamy mashed potatoes and buttered cabbage or spring greens.

Serves 4-5.

Left: Cornish Pasties.
Right: Midweek Meat Loaf.

ITALIAN LASAGNE

Adapt this recipe according to the occasion: if it is for a simple family supper, increase the amount of well-flavoured Cheddar cheese used, to take the place of the Jarlsberg cheese, which is similar to Swiss Emmenthal and Gruyère but is cheaper. It gives that traditional treacly texture to the cheese sauce.

This recipe serves six, as it is ideal for a dinner party, too. Lasagne is excellent to freeze when assembled, then you can simply thaw and bake it when needed.

Meat sauce

¾ lb (350g) minced beef
8 oz (225g) onions, chopped
1 level tbsp plain flour
½ pt (300ml) water
1 red Oxo cube, crumbled
3 rounded tbsp tomato purée
2 cloves of garlic, crushed
2 level tsp brown sugar
1 level tsp salt
Black pepper
4 oz (100g) mushrooms, chopped
8 oz (225g) chicken livers, chopped

White sauce

1½ oz (40g) butter
1½ oz (40g) plain flour
¼ tsp nutmeg
Salt and pepper
¾ pt (450ml) milk
½ level tsp made mustard
4 oz (100g) Cheddar cheese, grated
4 oz (100g) Jarlsberg or Emmenthal cheese, grated
½ oz (12½g) Parmesan cheese
5-6 oz (150-175g) uncooked lasagne

Cooking time: About 45-60 minutes.

To make the meat sauce: Heat the minced beef in a saucepan, slowly at first to allow the fat to run out, then fry until brown. Add the onions and cook for a further 5 minutes. Stir in the flour and all the remaining ingredients except the mushrooms and chicken livers, cover with a lid or foil and simmer for 45 minutes. Add the mushrooms and chicken livers and cook for a further 15 minutes. Taste and check seasoning.

To make the white sauce: Melt the butter in a saucepan, stir in the flour, nutmeg, salt and pepper and cook gently for 2 minutes. Remove the pan from the heat and gradually add the milk, stirring to make a smooth mixture. Return to the heat and cook, stirring constantly until the sauce has thickened. Add the mustard and check seasoning.

Combine the Cheddar and Jarlsberg cheeses.

In a shallow 3½ pt (2l) heatproof casserole, place one-third of the meat sauce, one-third of the white sauce and one-third of the cheese mixture, followed by half of the uncooked lasagne (arranged edge to edge, not over-lapping). Cover with another one-third of the meat sauce, white sauce and cheese and the remaining half of the lasagne. Finish with a final layer of meat sauce, white sauce and cheese mixture. Sprinkle over the Parmesan cheese. Leave to become cold.

When required, heat the oven to 350°F (180°C) mark 4. Cook for about 45-60 minutes or until the top is golden brown and bubbling. Serve immediately, or reduce the heat to 200°F (100°C) mark ¼ and keep warm for up to 1 hour.

Accompaniments: Serve this dish with a tossed green salad and French bread.

Serves 6.

Italian Lasagne.

BEEF WELLINGTON

Buy the puff pastry for this recipe as it gives very good results. Ideally the piece of fillet should be cut from the thick end as it carves better.

2 oz (50g) butter
2 lb (900g) beef fillet
2 large onions, sliced
4 oz (100g) mushrooms, sliced
1 tbsp chopped parsley
A pinch of thyme
½ level tsp salt
Black pepper
14 oz (397g) packet of puff pastry, thawed
A little beaten egg (to glaze)

Cooking time: About 1 hour.

Heat the oven to 425°F (220°C) mark 7.

Melt the butter in a frying pan, add the meat and fry quickly to brown, turning occasionally to seal in the juices on all sides. Lift it out and allow to cool.

Add the sliced onions to the pan and cook, stirring constantly, for about 5-10 minutes or until golden brown. Add the mushrooms and cook for a further 5 minutes. Stir in the parsley, thyme, salt and freshly ground pepper. Remove the pan from the heat and allow to cool.

Roll out the pastry on a lightly floured surface to a rectangle measuring about 14 x 16 in. (35 x 40cm), though this size may vary slightly with the shape of the piece of beef. Set the beef in the centre of the pastry and place the onion and mushroom mixture on top. Cut a 1½ in. (3.5cm) square from each corner of the pastry and keep on one side. Fold up the pastry around the meat, turning up the ends first and then the sides, which should just overlap the meat to cover it completely. Dampen the pastry with water or beaten egg where it overlaps so that it remains secure during cooking. Turn over, place on a baking sheet and brush the top with beaten egg. Cut the remaining pastry into leaf shapes and use to decorate the top. Brush with more beaten egg. Bake in the oven for about 1 hour if you like beef to be pink in the centre. Serve at once.

Accompaniments: Courgettes and sauté potatoes.

Serves 6.

BEEF GOULASH

This is a colourful casserole which you should cook slowly to bring out the flavour and richness.

1½ lb (675g) stewing steak
1 oz (25g) dripping
8 oz (225g) onions, sliced
2 level tbsp paprika pepper
1 oz (25g) plain flour
14 oz (397g) can of peeled tomatoes
½ pt (300ml) water
1 red Oxo cube
Salt and pepper
1 large green pepper, seeded and cut into strips

Cooking time: About 2½ hours.

Cut the meat into neat 1 in. (2.5cm) cubes. Melt the dripping in a saucepan and fry the meat for 3-4 minutes to quickly seal and brown. Lift it out with a slotted spoon and keep on one side. Add the onions to the pan and fry for 5 minutes to lightly brown. Stir in the paprika pepper and flour and cook for 1 minute. Add the tomatoes, water, crumbled Oxo cube, salt and pepper and bring to the boil, stirring until thickened. Return the meat to the pan, partially cover with a lid and simmer very gently for 1½ hours.

Add the green pepper and continue cooking for a further hour or until the meat is tender. Taste and check seasoning. Turn into a warm serving dish.

Accompaniments: This is tasty served piping hot with buttered noodles.

Serves 4-6.

Beef Wellington.

ORLANDO BEEF

This is a lovely rich, dark orange casserole when cooked. As it is quite spicy, it is not really suitable for children.

1½ lb (675g) stewing steak
1 oz (25g) beef dripping
1 lb (450g) onions, chopped
14 oz (397g) can of peeled tomatoes
1 level tsp curry powder
2 level tbsp tomato purée
1 tbsp vinegar
2 level tbsp apricot jam
¼ pt (150ml) water
1 red Oxo cube, crumbled
1 level tsp salt
Plenty of black pepper
1 bayleaf

Cooking time: About 2-3 hours.

Heat the oven to 325°F (160°C) mark 3.

Cut the beef into neat 1 in. (2.5cm) cubes. Melt the dripping in a large frying pan, add the beef and fry for 3-4 minutes to brown on all sides. Stir in the onions and fry for about 1 minute, turning them in the fat. Add all the remaining ingredients and bring to the boil, stirring until well blended. Turn into a 2½ pt (1.4l) heatproof casserole, cover with a lid or foil and cook in the oven for 2-3 hours or until the meat is tender. Taste and check seasoning. Remove the bayleaf.

Accompaniments: I like to serve this dish with plain boiled rice.

Serves 4-6.

Top: Orlando Beef.
Bottom: Mild Beef Curry.

MILD BEEF CURRY

This is one of my favourite curry recipes as it has such a good flavour. It may be adapted to use either small pieces of chicken or lean pork. It is essential to cook curries slowly to bring out their full flavour.

2 lb (900g) stewing steak
1½ oz (40g) plain flour
1½ tsp salt
1 large onion, peeled and chopped
2 oz (50g) margarine
1 level tbsp curry powder
1 level tbsp paprika pepper
½ pt (300ml) water
1 red Oxo cube, crumbled
2 dried red chilli peppers
1 tbsp mango chutney
1 tsp Worcestershire sauce
1 lb (454g) can of pineapple cubes
2 bayleaves

Cooking time: About 2 hours.

Trim any fat from the beef, cut the lean meat into neat ¾ in. (2cm) cubes and toss in the flour and salt. Place the onion in a saucepan with the margarine and fry gently for 5 minutes or until soft. Stir in the curry powder and paprika pepper and fry for a further 5 minutes. Stir in the pieces of beef, increase the heat and fry quickly to seal the juices. Add to the pan all the remaining ingredients including the pineapple syrup and bring to the boil, stirring until blended. Reduce the heat, cover with a lid and simmer very gently for about 2 hours or until the beef is really tender.

If preferred, the curry may be turned into a heatproof casserole and cooked in the oven at 325°F (160°C) mark 3 for about 2 hours.

Taste and check seasoning. Remove the bayleaves and chilli peppers.

Accompaniments: Serve with plain boiled rice and a selection of side dishes such as poppadoms, mango chutney, coconut, bananas, yogurt and sliced tomatoes and onions.

Serves 6-8.

ENGLISH RIB ROAST

I like to ask butchers which roast they would take home for their own family. Nine times out of ten the answer is fore rib of beef, as it is less expensive than sirloin and, to my mind, every bit as good.

Order the joint well in advance, so that it can be really well hung for a couple of weeks. Ask your butcher to saw off the vertebrae (but to leave them attached) and to remove the gristle which runs in a long line underneath. A joint of this kind, consisting of 3-4 ribs, will weigh about 12-14 lb (5.4-6.3kg), and is ideal served cold in this way at a party buffet.

1 fore rib of beef
Salt

Cooking time: About 2 hours 25 minutes-2 hours 36 minutes.

Heat the oven to 400°F (200°C) mark 6.

Rub a little salt over the fat on the beef and stand the ribs upright in a roasting tin. Roast in the oven for 12 minutes to the lb (450g) if you like beef pink in the centre but not dripping blood; or 13-14 minutes to the lb (450g) if you like it well done. Remove the meat from the oven and allow it to become quite cold. Chill in the refrigerator before carving.

Accompaniments: Serve with horseradish sauce (see page 58).

Serves 16-20 (or more if served with other meats as part of a buffet).

WALDORF BEEF SALAD

When the left-over cuts of beef joint are frankly not enough for four, serve them like this, with the meat cut into very fine strips.

4 hard dessert apples
3 sticks of celery
2 oz (50g) walnuts
4 tbsp mayonnaise
4 tbsp double or whipping cream, lightly whipped
A little lemon juice
Salt
Black pepper
8 oz (225g) cooked roast beef, cut into strips
Small sprigs of watercress (to garnish)

Wipe the apples. Leave them unpeeled, but quarter, core and cut them into small dice and put in a bowl. Finely slice the celery, coarsely chop the nuts and add them to the bowl.

Blend the mayonnaise with the cream, add the lemon juice and season with plenty of salt and freshly ground pepper. Stir into the apple mixture and mix thoroughly so the apples are well coated to prevent them from discolouring. Cover and leave to stand in a cool place for at least 1 hour to allow the flavours to blend.

When ready to serve, gently fold in the strips of beef. Pile into a serving dish and garnish with the watercress.

Accompaniments: Serve with baked potatoes.

Serves 4.

Top: English Rib Roast.
Bottom: Waldorf Beef Salad.

SAVOURY BEEF CRUMBLE

This is an excellent midweek meal which can be made in advance and reheated when required.

1 lb (450g) minced beef
2 onions, chopped
1½ oz (40g) plain flour
¾ pt (450ml) water
2 red Oxo cubes
Salt and pepper
2 large carrots, sliced

Topping
4 oz (100g) self-raising flour
1½ oz (40g) margarine
1 oz (25g) Cheddar cheese, grated
Salt and pepper
½ level tsp dry mustard
2 tomatoes, sliced
Paprika pepper

Cooking time: About 30 minutes.

Place the minced beef in a saucepan and cook gently for 5 minutes to allow the fat to run out. Add the onions and cook quickly for 2-3 minutes. Stir in the flour and cook for 1 minute. Add the water, crumbled Oxo cubes, salt, pepper and sliced carrots and bring to the boil, stirring constantly. Reduce the heat, cover with a lid and simmer for 45 minutes. Taste and check seasoning. Turn into a heatproof casserole.

Heat the oven to 350°F (180°C) mark 4.

Put the flour in a bowl, cut the margarine into small pieces and rub into the flour with the fingertips until the mixture resembles breadcrumbs. Stir in the cheese, salt, pepper and mustard. Spoon over the top of the mince and arrange slices of tomato around the edge of the dish. Sprinkle with paprika pepper. Cook in the oven for about 30 minutes or until the top is golden brown and crisp.

Accompaniments: Serve with creamy mashed potatoes and spring greens.

Serves 4.

BOILED SALT BEEF AND MUSTARD SAUCE

Order the silverside from your butcher at least a week in advance, as some butchers only keep brine for salting in the cold winter months. Take care to simmer the meat very slowly otherwise the joint will shrink.

3 lb (1.3kg) piece of boned and rolled silverside or brisket of beef
8 oz (225g) small carrots
8 oz (225g) small onions
2 oz (50g) butter
2 oz (50g) plain flour
½ pt (300ml) milk
1 level tbsp dry mustard
1 level tbsp soft, light brown sugar
3 tbsp vinegar
Salt and pepper

Cooking time: About 2 hours 20 minutes.

Wash the meat in cold water and, if necessary, soak overnight to remove any excess salt. Place the meat in a large saucepan, cover with cold water and bring to the boil. Cover with a lid or foil and simmer very gently for 35 minutes per lb (450g) plus an extra 35 minutes.

Peel the carrots and onions (leave them whole) and add them to the pan for the last hour of the meat's cooking time. Lift the meat onto a serving dish, remove the vegetables with a slotted spoon and arrange around the meat.

Melt the butter in a saucepan, add the flour and cook for 2 minutes. Stir in the milk and ½ pt (300ml) of cooking liquor and bring the sauce to the boil, stirring constantly. Simmer for 2 minutes to thicken. Blend together the mustard, sugar and vinegar and stir into the sauce. Cook for 1 minute, then add salt and pepper to taste.

Accompaniments: Serve with plain boiled potatoes and a green vegetable such as Brussels sprouts.

Serves 8.

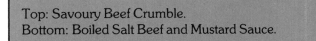

Top: Savoury Beef Crumble.
Bottom: Boiled Salt Beef and Mustard Sauce.

DEVILLED BEEF

A perfect midweek casserole to serve in winter, this dish has a thick rich gravy and is made with seasonings which most people always have in their store cupboard.

1½ lb (675g) stewing steak
1 oz (25g) dripping
8 oz (225g) small onions, quartered
1 oz (25g) plain flour
1 rounded tbsp tomato purée
1 tbsp Worcestershire sauce
1 level tbsp made mustard
1 tbsp honey
1 tbsp vinegar
About ¾ pt (450ml) water
1 red Oxo cube, crumbled
Salt and pepper

Cooking time: 2-2½ hours.

Cut the stewing steak into 1 in. (2.5cm) cubes. Melt the dripping in a saucepan, add the onions and meat and fry for 5 minutes, stirring frequently. Add the remaining ingredients and bring to the boil, stirring constantly. Reduce the heat, cover with a lid or foil and simmer very gently, stirring occasionally, for 2-2½ hours or until the meat is tender. Taste and check seasoning. Turn into a warm casserole and serve immediately.

Accompaniments: Serve either plain boiled or creamed potatoes and buttered cabbage or spring greens.

Serves 4-6.

Top: Devilled Beef.
Bottom: Crunchy Topped Mince.

CRUNCHY TOPPED MINCE

If you are making this dish in advance, simply cook the mince, then top with the fried bread croûtons just before serving. This is a good recipe for using up rather dried, hard cheese.

1 large onion, chopped
1 oz (25g) dripping or oil
1 lb (450g) minced beef
1 oz (25g) plain flour
1 level tsp salt
1 red Oxo cube
½ pt (300ml) hot water
1 tbsp Worcestershire sauce
Topping
4 slices white bread, medium sliced
2 oz (50g) butter
2 oz (50g) Cheddar cheese, grated

Cooking time: About 1¼ hours.

In a saucepan, fry the onion in the dripping until softened and beginning to brown. Add the meat, flour and salt and stir over fairly high heat to seal the meat. As the meat begins to brown, stir more frequently to prevent it from sticking to the pan. Cook for about 5 minutes. Mix the Oxo cube with the hot water and add the Worcestershire sauce. Stir this into the meat and bring to the boil. Cover with a lid or foil and simmer on low heat for about 1 hour, stirring occasionally. Place the cooked mince in a shallow heatproof dish and keep hot.

Cut the crusts off the bread and cut the rest into small dice about ¼ in. (0.6cm) square. Melt the butter in a frying pan and gently fry the bread, turning it to coat the croûtons with butter until lightly coloured and crisp. Remove from the heat, quickly stir in the cheese and immediately place all ingredients on top of the mince.

Accompaniments: Serve with a selection of colourful vegetables.

Serves 4.

EASY BEEF PIE

In winter, serve this hot with potatoes, carrots and onion gravy. In summer, serve it cold, cut into wedges.

Filling

1 level tbsp cornflour
1 red Oxo cube
4 tbsp water
¾ lb (350g) minced beef
1 small onion, grated
4 oz (100g) carrots, grated
½ level tsp dried mixed herbs
Salt and pepper

Pastry

8 oz (225g) plain flour
2 oz (50g) margarine
2 oz (50g) lard
About 2 tbsp cold water
Sprigs of parsley (to garnish)

Cooking time: About 50-60 minutes.

Heat the oven to 400°F (200°C) mark 6.

Put the cornflour, crumbled Oxo cube and water in a bowl. Stir until blended and smooth, add all the remaining filling ingredients and mix thoroughly.

To make the pastry: Put the flour in a bowl, cut the margarine and lard into small pieces and rub into the flour with the fingertips until the mixture resembles fine breadcrumbs. Add sufficient water to mix to a firm dough.

Roll out about two-thirds of the pastry on a lightly floured surface and use it to line a deep metal pie plate or flan ring 8 in. (20cm) in diameter. Place the filling in the pastry case, then roll out the remaining pastry. Dampen the edges of the pastry and use it to cover the top of the pie. Seal the edges securely and make a small slit in the centre of the pie to allow the steam to escape. Brush the top of the pie with a little milk to glaze. Bake in the oven for about 50-60 minutes or until the pastry is golden brown. Garnish with sprigs of parsley.

Serves 6.

FARMHOUSE BEEF

In this recipe, vinegar is used as the marinade and then in the cooking as it has a tenderising effect on the beef.

2 lb (900g) piece of topside of beef
1 onion, sliced
1 bayleaf
Salt
Black pepper
½ pt (300ml) white wine vinegar
¾ pt (450ml) cold water
1 oz (25g) dripping
1 brown bread crust (from the end of the loaf)
1 rounded tsp dark brown sugar
2 rounded tsp cornflour

Cooking time: About 1½ hours.

Put the meat in a china or glass bowl with the onion, bayleaf, salt and freshly ground pepper. Blend the vinegar with the water, pour over the beef, cover with foil and allow to stand in a cool place for 4-6 days, turning once a day.

Lift the meat from the marinade and pat thoroughly to dry.

Melt the dripping in a heavy saucepan, add the meat and fry quickly to brown all over. Strain off any excess dripping. Pour over ½ pt (300ml) of the marinade, add the crust of bread and sugar, cover with a lid or foil and simmer for 1½ hours or until the meat is tender.

Lift out the beef and place on a warm serving dish. Strain ½ pt (300ml) of the liquor from the pan into a measuring jug. Add the cornflour to the pan, blend with 2 tbsp of cold marinade and stir in the ½ pt (300ml) of hot stock. Return the pan to the heat and bring to the boil, stirring until smooth and thickened. Taste and check seasoning. Add a little extra sugar if necessary, as the sauce should be slightly sweet and sour. Pour into a sauce boat and serve with the beef.

Accompaniments: Serve with plain boiled potatoes and buttered carrots.

Serves 6.

Top: Farmhouse Beef marinating in vinegar.
Bottom: Easy Beef Pie.

BEEF STROGANOF

It is essential to use rump steak for this recipe, as the cooking time is very short. Don't cook the dish in advance: prepare the ingredients and cook as required.

1 lb (450g) rump steak
3 oz (75g) butter
2 onions, chopped
6 oz (175g) button mushrooms, sliced
4 tomatoes, skinned, seeded and chopped
Salt
Black pepper
½ pt (300ml) soured cream

Cooking time: About 12 minutes.

Cut the beef into thin strips about 2 x ½ in. (5 x 1.25cm). Melt half of the butter in a frying pan, add the onions and fry for about 5 minutes or until soft. Add the mushrooms and tomatoes and cook for a further 2-3 minutes. Lift them out of the pan with a slotted spoon and keep warm on one side. Add the remaining butter to the pan and quickly fry the strips of steak for about 4 minutes or until lightly cooked. Return the vegetables to the pan and season well with salt and freshly ground pepper. Reduce the heat, stir in the soured cream and reheat but do not boil. Taste and check seasoning. Turn into a warm serving dish and serve immediately.

Accompaniments: Serve with plain boiled rice and a vegetable such as broccoli spears tossed in butter, ratatouille, courgettes or French beans.

Serves 4.

Top: Bœuf Bourguignonne.
Bottom: Beef Stroganof.

BŒUF BOURGUIGNONNE

No meat cookery book would be complete without this classic French wine casserole, which is particularly good for winter entertaining.

1½ lb (675g) chuck steak
6 oz (175g) streaky bacon
½ oz (12½g) plain flour
¼ pt (150ml) water
½ pt (300ml) inexpensive Burgundy
1 red Oxo cube
1 bayleaf
½ level tsp dried mixed herbs
Salt and pepper
12 small pickling onions
6 oz (175g) button mushrooms
Chopped parsley (to garnish)

Cooking time: About 2½ hours.

Cut the beef into 1½ in. (3.5cm) cubes. Cut the rind, fatty pieces and any bones from the bacon, and cut the lean bacon across into small strips. Place the bacon rind and fat in a saucepan and cook gently for 3-4 minutes to allow the fat to run out. Lift out the rind and discard it. Leave the fat in the pan and fry the bacon strips and beef until browned. Lift them out with a slotted spoon and place in a heatproof casserole about 3 pt (1.7l) in capacity.

Heat the oven to 325°F (160°C) mark 3.

Stir the flour into the fat remaining in the pan and cook for 1 minute. Stir in the water, wine, crumbled Oxo cube, bayleaf, herbs, salt and pepper and bring to the boil, stirring constantly. Pour into the casserole. Cover with a lid or foil and cook in the oven for 1½ hours.

Peel the onions (leave them whole) and add to the casserole with the mushrooms. Cook for a further hour or until the meat is really tender. Taste and check seasoning. Remove the bayleaf. If necessary, skim off any excess fat. Sprinkle with chopped parsley and serve straight from the dish in which it was cooked.

Accompaniments: Serve with new potatoes and braised celery.

Serves 4-6.

SPAGHETTI BOLOGNESE

Many greengrocers sell mushroom stalks at half the price of whole mushrooms, and they are ideal to use in a recipe like this. Simply slice them and stir into the sauce as usual; they have an excellent flavour. If they are dirty, put them in a sieve and run them under the cold tap.

1 tbsp oil
2 medium onions, chopped
1 lb (450g) minced beef
1 clove of garlic, crushed
1½ oz (40g) plain flour
1 rounded tbsp tomato purée
½ pt (300ml) water
2 red Oxo cubes
14 oz (397g) can of peeled tomatoes
1 level tsp salt
Black pepper
4 oz (100g) mushroom stalks or mushrooms, sliced
12 oz (350g) spaghetti
Parmesan or Cheddar cheese, finely grated (to serve)

Cooking time: About 1 hour.

Heat the oil in a saucepan and fry the onions, beef and garlic for 5 minutes. Stir in the flour and cook for 1 minute. Add the tomato purée, water and crumbled Oxo cubes and bring to the boil, stirring constantly. Add the tomatoes and season well with salt and freshly ground pepper. Reduce the heat, partially cover with a lid and simmer for about 45 minutes. Stir in the mushroom stalks or mushrooms and cook for a further 15 minutes or until the beef is tender. Taste and check seasoning. Add a little more water if necessary.

Meanwhile cook the spaghetti in plenty of fast boiling, salted water as directed on the packet. The spaghetti should be slightly firm to the bite but not hard in the centre. Strain through a colander and rinse in warm water. Rinse out the saucepan, add a little oil, return the spaghetti to the pan and toss gently to coat evenly. Turn the spaghetti onto individual plates and spoon the sauce into the middle. Serve the cheese separately in a small bowl.

Serves 4-6.

LATIMER BEEF

This is a special casserole and one that I make time and time again as it is unusual and spicy. It is particularly suitable if you are entertaining and want to make it in advance.

1½ lb (675g) stewing steak
1 oz (25g) beef dripping
8 oz (225g) onions, chopped
1 oz (25g) plain flour
1 level tsp curry powder
1 level tsp ground ginger
½ pt (300ml) water
1 red Oxo cube
1 rounded tsp salt
Plenty of black pepper
1 level tbsp brown sugar
1 tbsp Worcestershire sauce
2 rounded tbsp horseradish cream (the bottled variety)
Fresh, chopped chives or parsley

Cooking time: About 2½-3 hours.

Heat the oven to 325°F (160°C) mark 3.

Cut the meat into ¾ in. (1.8cm) cubes. Melt the dripping in a large saucepan, add the meat and brown on all sides. Add the onions, turning in the dripping, then add the spices and flour and mix well. Stir in the water and crumbled Oxo cube and bring to the boil. Season well with salt and freshly ground pepper. Add the sugar and Worcestershire sauce. Turn into a heatproof casserole, cover with a lid or foil and cook in the oven for 2½-3 hours or until the beef is tender. Shortly before serving, stir in the horseradish cream. Taste and check seasoning. Sprinkle with chopped chives or parsley.

Accompaniments: As this dish is cooked in the oven for 2-3 hours, you could cook some jacket potatoes and braised celery in the oven at the same time. However, the potato skins will not be crisp, because the oven temperature is too low. A milk pudding could be cooked on the lower shelf so you would have a meal cooked entirely in the oven.

Serves 4.

LAMB
RECIPES

Leg of lamb – a classic lamb roast (see pages 16-17 for roasting instructions). Serve with the traditional accompaniments of roast potatoes, mint sauce and gravy (see pages 55-60).

CAVALRY LAMB

Most butchers will prepare a guard of honour for you if given 24 hours' notice. It is made from two best ends of lamb with the tops of the bones trimmed clean to about 3 in. (7.5cm). The two pieces of meat are then joined and sewn together along the bottom meaty part of the joints, with the skin outermost. The meat is then folded together, with the skin on the outside so that the cleaned bones meet and cross at the top. The bones may be protected with foil when cooking to prevent them from burning.

Stuffing

2 oz (50g) dried apricots
1 oz (25g) butter
1 medium onion, chopped
1 oz (25g) almonds, chopped
4 oz (100g) long-grain rice
Salt and pepper
¾ pt (450ml) water

1 prepared guard of honour

Cooking time: About 40 minutes.

Finely chop the apricots and put them in a small bowl. Cover with water and allow to soak for several hours or overnight.

Heat the oven to 400°F (200°C) mark 6.

To prepare the stuffing: Melt the butter in a small saucepan and fry the onion for about 5 minutes or until soft. Add the almonds and fry for 2-3 minutes to brown. Drain the apricots and add them to the pan with the rice, salt and pepper. Add the water and simmer gently until all the water has been absorbed and the rice is tender (about 15-20 minutes or until cooked. This will vary slightly with the variety of rice used.) Taste and check seasoning. Put the stuffing in the centre of the lamb, place the lamb in a roasting tin and roast in the oven for about 40 minutes or until tender. Decorate with a cutlet frill on top of each bone and lift onto a serving dish.

Accompaniments: Serve with a thin gravy and mint sauce (see pages 58 and 55) or redcurrant jelly. Cauliflower in white sauce and roast potatoes are very good with lamb.

Serves 6.

SPICY LAMB

This casserole has a mild curry flavour, and makes a tasty meal for all the family. The carrots and onions give it a colourful appearance.

1½ lb (675g) boneless fillet, leg or shoulder of lamb
1½ oz (40g) plain flour
2 level tsp mild curry powder
1½ level tsp salt
Black pepper
2 tbsp oil
1 pt (600ml) water
2 chicken Oxo cubes
8 oz (225g) button onions, peeled and left whole
8 oz (225g) small carrots, quartered lengthwise

Cooking time: About 1¼ hours.

Trim any excess fat from the lamb and cut the lean meat into 1 in. (2.5cm) cubes. Put the flour, curry powder, salt and freshly ground pepper in a bag, add the lamb and shake well to coat it thoroughly with the seasoned flour.

Heat the oil in a saucepan, add the lamb and fry for 2-3 minutes. Stir in the remaining flour, add the water and crumbled Oxo cubes and bring to the boil, stirring constantly. Add the onions and carrots, cover with a lid and simmer very gently for about 1¼ hours or until the lamb and vegetables are tender. Taste and check seasoning. Turn into a warm dish and serve immediately.

Accompaniments: Serve with plain boiled rice and the usual curry accompaniments such as poppadoms and chutney.

Serves 4-6.

Cavalry Lamb.

ROAST SADDLE OF LAMB

A saddle of lamb consists of the two loins joined together from ribs to tail. The kidneys are often attached to the saddle and may be roasted and served with the joint, a slice being given to each guest. For six people you would need a saddle about 6-7 lb (2.7-3.4kg) in weight.

1 saddle of young lamb (about 6-7 lb [2.7-3.4kg] in weight)
2 oz (50g) butter
2 sprigs of fresh rosemary
Salt and pepper

Gravy
2 tbsp fat (after roasting the meat)
1 oz (25g) plain flour
1 red Oxo cube
½ pt (300ml) hot water
1 rounded tsp redcurrant jelly
3 tbsp sherry
Salt and pepper

Cooking time: About 2 hours 55 minutes for a 6 lb (2.7kg) saddle.

Heat the oven to 375°F (190°C) mark 5.

Spread the butter over the joint, place the rosemary on top and season well with salt and pepper. Place in a roasting tin and cover with foil. Roast for 25 minutes to the lb (450g) plus an extra 25 minutes. Remove the foil after the first half hour of cooking time. Lift out the joint and place on a warm serving dish.

To make the gravy: Strain off most of the fat from the roasting tin, leaving 2 tbsp of the sediment. Stir in the flour and blend thoroughly with the fat. Cook on the hob for

2-3 minutes until brown, stirring constantly. Crumble the Oxo cube in the hot water and stir. Remove the pan from the heat and slowly add the stock. Return to the heat, bring to the boil and stir constantly until the gravy has thickened. Add the redcurrant jelly and sherry and season with salt and pepper to taste. Allow the jelly to dissolve, then pour into a sauce boat and serve with the joint.

Accompaniments: Braised celery and roast potatoes can be cooked in the oven beside the meat and, as it is a special dish, serve another vegetable such as Brussels sprouts.

Serves 6.

GLAZED MINT CHOPS

A simple and delicious way to serve chops.

4 lamb chops
Mint jelly
4 large tomatoes, halved
Sprigs of watercress or parsley (to garnish)

Cooking time: About 16-20 minutes.

Heat the grill to moderate and remove the rack from the grill pan.

Place the chops in the grill pan and spread 1 heaped tsp of mint jelly on each chop. Cook under the grill for 8-10 minutes, then turn the chops over and spread each one with another tsp of mint jelly. Add the halved tomatoes to the grill pan.

Continue cooking for a further 8-10 minutes until the chops are tender and have a lovely glaze. Watch the chops carefully, as the cooking time will vary slightly with the thickness of the chops. Remove from the grill pan and arrange on a warm serving dish. Garnish with sprigs of watercress or parsley.

Accompaniments: French or runner beans and tiny new potatoes cooked with a large sprig of mint are ideal with these chops.

Serves 4.

Top: Roast Saddle of Lamb.
Bottom: Glazed Mint Chops.

MOUSSAKA

I blanch the aubergines in water instead of frying them, because they are then far less fatty than when prepared in the traditional way.

1-1½ lb (450-675g) minced lamb (half a shoulder of lamb will give this)
8 oz (225g) onions, chopped
2 cloves of garlic, crushed
1½ oz (40g) plain flour
1½ level tsp salt
Black pepper
14 oz (397g) can of peeled tomatoes
3 aubergines

Sauce

1½ oz (40g) butter
1½ oz (40g) flour
¾ pt (450ml) milk
1 level tsp made mustard
Grated nutmeg
Salt and pepper
6 oz (175g) Cheddar cheese, grated
1 egg, beaten

Cooking time: About 45 minutes.

Heat the oven to 375°F (190°C) mark 5.

Butter a heatproof dish (about 3 pt [1.7l] capacity). Place the lamb in a large saucepan and cook over low heat at first to let the fat run out. Stir the meat to prevent it from sticking to the pan. Add the onions and garlic, increase the heat and fry for about 15 minutes to brown the meat. If after this time there seems to be an excess of fat, spoon off the surplus. Add the flour and stir well. Add the salt, freshly ground pepper and tomatoes. Bring to the boil and simmer for 5 minutes. Taste and check seasoning.

Cut the aubergines into ¼ in. (0.6cm) slices and blanch in a pan of boiling water for 1 minute. (This will soften the skins and prevent the aubergines from discolouring.) Drain in a colander, then dry on kitchen paper.

To make the sauce: Slowly melt the butter in a saucepan, add the flour and cook for a few minutes over moderate heat without colouring. Slowly blend in the milk and bring to the boil, stirring well. Add the mustard, nutmeg, salt, pepper and cheese. Heat until the cheese melts, then remove from the heat. Cool slightly, add the egg and mix well.

To assemble the moussaka: Arrange half of the meat mixture in the bottom of the dish, cover with half the aubergines and season with salt and pepper. Repeat with the rest of the lamb and aubergines, thus making four layers. Pour over the cheese sauce. Bake uncovered in the oven for 45 minutes-1 hour or until the moussaka is golden brown.

Accompaniments: Serve with hot French bread and, if liked, a green salad.

Serves 6-8.

LAMB KEBABS

Lamb is delicious cooked in this way. It is essential to use really fresh small button mushrooms; if they are too large they look out of place.

Marinade

1 teacup of olive oil
1 glass of inexpensive red wine
1 clove of garlic, crushed
1 sprig of fresh rosemary or 1 level tsp rubbed rosemary
1 level tsp fresh or dried basil
Salt and black pepper

2 lb (900g) lean leg of lamb
1 medium onion (optional)
1 red pepper
1 green pepper
8 small, firm tomatoes, halved
8 button mushrooms
Small pieces of bayleaf

Top: Moussaka.
Bottom: Lamb Kebabs.

Lamb Kebabs continued from page 109.

Cooking time: About 15 minutes.

Mix together all the marinade ingredients. Cut the lamb into 1½ in. (3.5cm) cubes and add it to the marinade. Cover with foil and leave in the refrigerator overnight.

Cut the onion (if used) and peppers into quarters. Take 8 long skewers and oil them well. Use the skewers to pierce the meat alternately with pieces of the vegetables and bayleaf.

Heat the grill to hot.

Place the kebabs in the grill pan, baste with some of the marinade and grill for about 10 minutes, turning frequently and basting so that the meat does not scorch. Arrange the kebabs on a warm serving dish and serve at once.

Accompaniments: Serve the kebabs on a bed of saffron or savoury rice.

Serves 4.

LAMB CHOPS WITH RATATOUILLE

Make this dish in the summer when courgettes and tomatoes are plentiful, particularly if you grow your own.

1 green pepper
1 red pepper
3 tbsp oil
1 large onion, sliced
1 clove of garlic, crushed
4 chump chops
12 oz (350g) courgettes, sliced
12 oz (350g) tomatoes, peeled and quartered
Salt and black pepper

Cooking time: About 30 minutes.

Remove the core and seeds from the peppers and cut into strips. Heat the oil in a saucepan and add the peppers, onion and garlic. Cover with a lid or foil and cook gently for about 15 minutes until soft but not brown.

Meanwhile lightly fry the chops in a frying pan for about 10

minutes or until well browned on both sides.

Add the courgettes and tomatoes to the saucepan with the salt and freshly ground pepper and stir well. Arrange the chops on top and cook uncovered over gentle heat for about 15 minutes. Taste and check seasoning. Turn into a hot serving dish and serve immediately.

Accompaniments: Serve with chunks of French bread.

Serves 4.

IRISH STEW

True Irish stew is made using only lamb and potatoes, but I include carrots too. If you dislike bones, make the stew with neck fillet of lamb, allow 1 lb (450g) for four people and cut it into neat 1 in. (2.5cm) cubes.

2½ lb (1.1kg) middle neck of lamb
2 large onions
8 oz (225g) carrots (optional)
1 lb (450g) potatoes
Salt and black pepper
Chopped parsley (to garnish)

Cooking time: About 3 hours.

Heat the oven to 325°F (160°C) mark 3.

Cut the lamb into neat pieces and remove the spinal cord. Peel and slice the onions, carrots (if used) and potatoes. Arrange alternate layers of meat with layers of each vegetable in a 3 pt (1.7l) heatproof casserole, seasoning each layer with plenty of salt and freshly ground pepper. Finish with a layer of potato, which should be neatly arranged to give an attractive appearance to the finished dish. Pour in sufficient water to half-fill the casserole. Cover with a lid and bake in the oven for 2½ hours or until the meat is nearly tender.

Remove the lid, increase the oven temperature to 350°F (180°C) mark 4 and cook for a further 30 minutes or until the potatoes are pale brown.

Accompaniments: This casserole is a meal in itself but a green vegetable such as cabbage or sprouts can be served with it.

Serves 4.

ALGERIAN LAMB

A good dish to serve when entertaining friends, as it is so easy to carve.

1 small shoulder of lamb, boned and rolled
Salt and pepper
3 oz (75g) raisins
3 tbsp sherry
1 large onion, chopped
1 clove of garlic, crushed
1 level tbsp plain flour
½ level tsp turmeric
¼ level tsp chilli powder
14 oz (397g) can of peeled tomatoes
¼ pt (150ml) water
1 red Oxo cube

Cooking time: About 1¾ hours.

Heat the oven to 375°F (190°C) mark 5.

Place the lamb in a roasting tin and season well with salt and pepper. Roast in the oven for about 1¾ hours or for 30 minutes to the lb (450g) plus an extra 30 minutes.

Meanwhile put the raisins and sherry in a small bowl and allow to soak throughout the meat's cooking time.

Lift out the meat, place on a serving dish and keep warm. Pour off most of the fat from the roasting tin, leaving about 2 tbsp of the sediment. Add the onion and garlic and fry for about 5 minutes or until golden brown. Stir in the flour, turmeric and chilli powder and cook for a further 2 minutes. Add the tomatoes, water, crumbled Oxo cube, raisins and sherry and bring to the boil, stirring constantly until the sauce has thickened. Reduce the heat and simmer for about 5 minutes. Taste and check seasoning. Serve with the lamb.

Accompaniments: Serve with boiled potatoes, parsnips and buttered cabbage.

Serves 6-8.

TUESDAY'S POTATO LAYER PIE

Use the last trimmings from the family's Sunday joint for this recipe. Add any mint sauce that may be left over too, because it gives a lovely flavour. If you haven't got quite 12 oz (350g) of meat, it doesn't matter: simply add some more vegetable.

About 12 oz (350g) cooked roast lamb
2 carrots
1 large onion
¼ level tsp dried mixed herbs
1 level tsp salt
Black pepper
1 lb (450g) potatoes
1 oz (25g) lamb dripping
1 red Oxo cube
½ pt (300ml) hot water

Cooking time: About 1 hour.

Heat the oven to 350°F (180°C) mark 4.

Mince together the lamb, carrots and onion. Mix with the herbs, salt and freshly ground pepper (and about 2 tsp of mint sauce, if you have any left over). Peel and thinly slice the potatoes.

Cover the bottom of a deep 3 pt (1.7l) heatproof casserole with half of the dripping. Arrange one-third of the potato slices over the bottom of the dish, cover with half of the meat mixture, add another layer of potatoes, then the remaining meat, and finally a neatly arranged topping of potato slices (keep the biggest and best slices for the top). Crumble the Oxo cube in the hot water, stir and pour into the casserole. Dot the top of the potatoes with the remaining dripping, cover with a lid or foil and bake in the oven for about 1 hour. Remove the lid and place the casserole under a hot grill for 5 minutes to brown and crisp the top layer of potatoes.

Accompaniments: Serve with young spring greens or a green salad.

Serves 4.

NAVARIN OF LAMB

Navarin is a French cooking term for a casserole of lamb or mutton and vegetables.

2 lb (900g) middle neck of lamb, cut into pieces
1 oz (25g) plain flour
2 oz (50g) dripping
1 pt (600ml) water
2 level tbsp tomato purée
1 red Oxo cube
1 lb (450g) small young carrots, sliced
8 oz (225g) button onions, peeled
Salt and pepper
12 small new potatoes

Cooking time: About 1¾ hours.

Heat the oven to 325°F (160°C) mark 3.

Trim any excess fat from the lamb and coat the lean meat in the flour. Heat the dripping in a large frying pan and quickly fry the meat to brown on both sides. Lift it out and place in a large 4½ pt (2.5l) heatproof casserole.

Stir any remaining flour into the fat in the frying pan and cook for 2 minutes. Add the water and tomato purée and bring to the boil, stirring constantly. Add the crumbled Oxo cube and simmer gently to thicken.

Add the carrots and onions to the casserole and pour over the sauce. Season well with salt and pepper, cover with a tight-fitting lid and cook in the oven for 1 hour.

Add the potatoes, ensuring that they are well pushed down into the sauce. Return to the oven and cook for a further 45 minutes or until the meat and vegetables are tender. Taste and check seasoning. Serve immediately.

Serves 4.

Top: Navarin of Lamb.
Bottom: Lamb Boulangère.

LAMB BOULANGÈRE

Carrots are a colourful vegetable to serve with lamb, and it is a good idea to serve casseroled carrots with this dish. They can be prepared and put in the oven beside the meat after the first hour's cooking time, and the meal is thus cooked entirely in the oven.

1 small leg of lamb
2 cloves of garlic
1 sprig of fresh rosemary
1½ lb (675g) potatoes
8 oz (225g) onions
Salt and pepper
½ pt (300ml) hot water
1 red Oxo cube
A little chopped parsley

Heat the oven to 375°F (190°C) mark 5.

Trim any excess fat from the lamb. Peel the garlic, cut it into thin slivers and press them into the lamb. Tie the sprig of rosemary over the lamb. Peel the potatoes and cut into thick slices. Peel and thinly slice the onions and mix with the potatoes. Place them in a shallow heatproof dish, season well with salt and pepper and arrange the lamb on top. Crumble the Oxo cube, blend with the hot water and pour over the meat and vegetables. Cover with foil and roast in the oven for 30 minutes per lb (450g) plus an extra 30 minutes.

After the first hour remove the foil, baste the meat and vegetables and return them to the oven to continue cooking. When the meat is cooked, untie the rosemary and place a fresh sprig on top. Sprinkle the vegetables with chopped parsley and serve straight from the dish in which it was cooked.

Accompaniments: Serve with casseroled carrots or a green vegetable such as peas or beans.

Serves 6-8.

SCOTTISH MUTTON PIES

Cold roast mutton or lamb is not usually very inspiring, but these tasty pies turn a small amount of lamb into a mid-week meal for four. If you want to try this recipe, serve roast lamb or boiled mutton with onion sauce at the weekend. Make twice as much sauce as you need and put some aside to make these pies. Onion sauce is especially good to serve with lamb in the winter months when there is no fresh mint about.

Filling

¾ oz (19g) butter
4 oz (100g) onions, chopped
¾ oz (19g) plain flour
¼ pt (150ml) milk
1 chicken Oxo cube
2-3 tbsp gravy or meat jelly
6 oz (175g) cooked lamb or mutton, diced
Salt and pepper

Shortcrust pastry

8 oz (225g) plain flour
2 oz (50g) margarine
2 oz (50g) lard
About 3 tbsp cold water

Cooking time: About 40 minutes.

To make the filling: Melt the butter in a small saucepan, add the onions and cook gently for about 10 minutes or until they are soft but not brown. Stir in the flour and cook for 1 minute. Add the milk, crumbled Oxo cube and gravy or meat jelly and simmer for 2 minutes. Remove the pan from the heat, add the lamb and season with salt and pepper. Allow to become quite cold.

To make the pastry: Put the flour in a bowl, cut the margarine and lard into small pieces and rub into the flour with the fingertips until the mixture resembles fine bread-crumbs. Add sufficient cold water to mix to a firm dough. Wrap and chill in the refrigerator for 30 minutes.

Heat the oven to 400°F (200°C) mark 6.

Roll out two-thirds of the pastry on a lightly floured surface and cut into 4 circles, each measuring 5 in. (12.5cm) in dia-meter. Use these to line 4 foil dishes or pie tins. Divide the filling equally between the pastry cases and brush the edges of the pastry with milk. Roll out the remaining pastry on a lightly floured surface and cut into 4 circles. Cover the pies with these pastry lids and seal the edges firmly with the prongs of a fork. Make a small slit in the centre of each pie, brush the tops with a little milk and bake in the oven for about 40 minutes or until golden brown.

Accompaniments: Carrots and Brussels sprouts are delicious with these pies.

Serves 4.

SCOTTISH STOVIES

For this Scottish dish the cooked lamb is usually finely chopped rather than minced. It is best made in a shallow pan, like a frying pan with a lid. If you like a brown top, remove the lid, brush with a little melted butter and slip the pan under the grill.

¾ lb (350g) cooked lamb
1 lb (450g) potatoes
1 large onion
Salt and pepper
1 red Oxo cube
About ½ pt (300ml) hot water

Cooking time: About 25-30 minutes.

Dice or mince the lamb. Peel and thinly slice the potatoes and onion. Fill the pan with alternate layers of potato, meat and onion, seasoning each layer with salt and pepper. Finish with a layer of potatoes, neatly arranged on top. Crumble the Oxo cube in the hot water and stir. Pour over the potatoes and cover with a lid. Simmer gently for 25-30 minutes, by which time the vegetables should be tender and most of the stock absorbed. However, if there is still quite a lot of stock left, remove the lid, increase the heat and boil rapidly for 2-3 minutes.

Serves 4.

Top: Scottish Stovies.
Bottom: Scottish Mutton Pies.

CROWN ROAST

A crown roast of lamb consists of two pieces of best end of neck of lamb, which are chined and then tied or sewn together, with a space being left in the centre for the stuffing. There are usually 12-14 cutlets in a crown. Give your butcher 24 hours' notice and he will prepare the crown for you.

1 crown of lamb
Salt and pepper

Stuffing
3 oz (75g) long-grain rice
1 oz (25g) butter
1 large onion, chopped
4 oz (100g) mushrooms, chopped
1 level tbsp fresh, chopped mixed herbs or parsley
Salt and pepper
1 egg, beaten

Watercress (to garnish)

Cooking time: About 1¾-2 hours.

Heat the oven to 350°F (180°C) mark 4.

If there is a piece of fat in the centre of the crown, remove this and discard it. Place the joint in a roasting tin and season well with salt and pepper. Wrap the end of each bone in foil to prevent them from burning during cooking.

To make the stuffing: Cook the rice in fast boiling, salted water for 10-12 minutes or as directed on the packet. Rinse in warm water and drain very thoroughly. Melt the butter in a small saucepan, add the onion and cook gently for about 8 minutes or until soft but not brown. Add the mushrooms and cook for 2 minutes. Remove the pan from the heat, stir in the rice and herbs and season with plenty of salt and pepper. Add the egg to bind and mix thoroughly. Pack into

Crown Roast.

the centre of the joint and cover the stuffing with a small piece of foil or buttered paper.

Roast in the oven for about 1¾ hours or for 25 minutes to the lb (450g), until the meat is tender and the juices run clear. Arrange on a serving dish and remove the foil from the stuffing and tips of the bones. Decorate each bone with a cutlet frill and garnish the dish with watercress. Serve 2 chops per person with the stuffing.

Accompaniments: Serve with mint jelly, gravy, roast potatoes and braised celery.

Serves 6-7.

PIQUANT LAMB CHOPS

Here's a different, spicy way of serving lamb chops. Use any chutney you have to hand in the store cupboard, especially if it is home-made.

A little marjoram
4 loin chops of lamb
Salt and pepper
About 3-4 tbsp chutney
4 rashers of back bacon (with rind removed)
Sprigs of watercress (to garnish)

Cooking time: About 30 minutes.

Heat the oven to 425°F (220°C) mark 7.

Sprinkle the marjoram on both sides of the chops, season well with salt and pepper and spread both sides of each chop with chutney. Wrap a rasher of bacon around each chop and secure with a wooden cocktail stick.

Place a rack in a roasting tin and arrange the chops on top. Cook in the oven for about 30 minutes, turning once, until the chops are tender (this will vary slightly with the thickness of the chops). Remove the cocktail sticks. Arrange on a warm serving dish, garnish with sprigs of watercress and serve immediately.

Accompaniments: Serve with Duchesse potatoes and whole baked tomatoes.

Serves 4.

SWEET AND SOUR LAMB WITH APRICOTS

Fillet of lamb lies at the base of the bones in the scrag end of neck, so you will have to buy a scrag end to get the fillet, although you can always use the bones to make Scotch broth. Take out the fillet in a long strip with a sharp knife. Alternatively, you can buy fillet of neck, although not all butchers sell it, or meat from a boned shoulder of lamb, cut into cubes.

1½ lb (675g) fillet of lamb
1 oz (25g) dripping
2 onions, chopped
2 level tsp paprika pepper
1 oz (25g) plain flour
½ pt (300ml) water
1 red Oxo cube
1 level tsp brown sugar
1 tbsp vinegar
Salt and pepper
7½ oz (213g) can of apricots, drained and sliced
Chopped parsley (to garnish)

Cooking time: About 1½ hours.

Cut the lamb into 2 in. (5cm) cubes. Place in a saucepan with the dripping and fry over moderate heat for 5 minutes. Add the onions and paprika to the pan and cook for 1 minute. Stir in the flour and cook for 2 minutes. Add the water, crumbled Oxo cube, sugar, vinegar, salt and pepper. Bring to the boil, stirring until thickened.

Cover with a lid or foil and simmer gently for 1 hour. Add the apricots and continue cooking for a further 30 minutes or until the lamb is tender. Turn into a warm serving dish and serve sprinkled with chopped parsley.

Accompaniments: Serve with noodles or pasta shells tossed in soured cream, and a vegetable such as peas.

Serves 4.

Left: Apricot Stuffed Lamb.
Right: Sweet and Sour Lamb with Apricots.

APRICOT STUFFED LAMB

Boning and stuffing a shoulder of lamb makes the meat go much further and makes carving so simple. Most butchers will remove the bones for you if they are not too busy

3½ lb (1.5kg) shoulder of lamb, boned
Salt and pepper
Stuffing
1 oz (25g) butter
1 onion, chopped
4 oz (100g) fresh brown breadcrumbs
1 tbsp fresh, chopped mint
2 oz (50g) raisins
1 large cooking apple, diced, peeled and cored
7½ oz (213g) can of apricots
1 egg, beaten
Salt and pepper

Cooking time: About 1¾ hours.

Heat the oven to 375°F (190°C) mark 5.

Open out the shoulder and season well with salt and pepper.

To make the stuffing: Melt the butter in a saucepan, add the onion, cover with a lid and cook gently for about 10 minutes or until the onion is soft but not brown. Remove from the heat and add the breadcrumbs, mint, raisins and apple. Drain the apricots, reserving the juice for the gravy. Chop the fruit and add to the stuffing with the egg, mix well and season with salt and pepper to taste. Use the stuffing to fill the cavity in the lamb, close with skewers to hold the stuffing in place and, if necessary, tie with fine string.

Place the shoulder in a roasting tin and roast in the oven for about 1¾ hours or 30 minutes to the lb (450g). Remove from the oven and place on a warm serving dish. Serve with a gravy made from the apricot syrup (see page 59).

Accompaniments: Serve the lamb with roast potatoes, mint jelly and cauliflower in white sauce.

Serves 8.

LANCASHIRE HOT POT

An ideal dish to leave in the oven to cook by itself while you are out.

2 lb (900g) middle neck of lamb
2 lambs' kidneys
½ oz (12½g) plain flour
2 onions, sliced
4 oz (100g) mushrooms, quartered
Salt and pepper
1½ lb (675g) potatoes, sliced
1 red Oxo cube
¾ pt (450ml) hot water
½ oz (12½g) dripping

Cooking time: About 2½ hours.

Heat the oven to 350°F (180°C) mark 4.

Wipe the lamb and cut into evenly-sized pieces. Cut the kidneys in half and peel off the skin. Use scissors to remove the core from each kidney. Cut into slices. Coat the lamb with the flour.

Place the onions in a 4 pt (2.3l) heatproof casserole and arrange the lamb, kidneys and mushrooms on top. Season well with salt and pepper. Arrange the potato slices on top. Crumble the Oxo cube in the hot water, stir and pour over the potatoes. Dot the potatoes with the dripping, cover with a lid or foil and cook in the oven for 2 hours.

Remove the lid or foil, return to the oven and cook for a further 30 minutes to allow the potatoes on top to brown.

Accompaniments: I serve this dish with a green vegetable such as Brussels sprouts, cabbage or spring greens.

Serves 4.

Top: Lancashire Hot Pot.
Bottom: Crispy Rack of Lamb.

CRISPY RACK OF LAMB

A rack of lamb consists of lamb chops in one piece with the chine bones removed so that it is easy to carve.

1 piece of best end of neck of lamb (about 6-7 cutlets)
Salt and pepper
8 oz (225g) carrots
1 large onion
Butter
½ pt (300ml) hot water
1 red Oxo cube
2 oz (50g) fresh white breadcrumbs
1 level tbsp chopped parsley

Cooking time: About 40 minutes.

Heat the oven to 450°F (230°C) mark 8.

Wrap the ends of each rib bone in foil to prevent them from burning while cooking. Season well with salt and pepper.

Coarsely mince or dice the carrots and onion and arrange in the bottom of a heatproof dish. Season with salt and pepper and dot with a little butter. Place the lamb, fat side down, on top of the vegetables and cook in the oven for 20 minutes. Reduce the oven temperature to 400°F (200°C) mark 6 and turn the lamb over so that the fat side is uppermost. Blend together the water and Oxo cube and pour over the vegetables. Mix the breadcrumbs with the parsley and pat firmly into the fat on the lamb. Return to the oven and cook for a further 20 minutes or until the lamb is golden brown and crisp.

Lift the lamb out of the dish and place on a warm serving plate. Serve the vegetables and stock with the rack of lamb. (If preferred, purée the vegetables and stock in a blender until quite smooth. Turn into a saucepan and reheat. Taste and check seasoning. Serve with the lamb.)

Accompaniments: Serve with mint jelly, Brussels sprouts and Duchesse potatoes.

Serves 3-4.

LAMB NOISETTE ROAST

This looks like a small roast and consists of best end chops which are left in one piece, then boned and rolled. It is very succulent and simple to carve.

Stuffing
1 oz (25g) butter
1 onion, chopped
4 oz (100g) mushrooms, chopped
2 oz (50g) fresh white breadcrumbs
Salt and pepper
1 small egg, beaten

1 piece of best end of neck (about 6 or 7 cutlets), boned
A little dripping

Cooking time: About 1 hour.

Heat the oven to 400°F (200°C) mark 6.

To prepare the stuffing: Melt the butter in a small saucepan, add the onion and cook gently for about 10 minutes or until the onion is soft but not brown. Add the mushrooms and cook for a further 3-4 minutes. Remove the pan from the heat and stir in the breadcrumbs, salt, pepper and sufficient beaten egg to bind.

Place the meat flat on a board and spread the stuffing down the centre. Roll up and secure the joint, tying firmly with string at 1 in. (2.5cm) intervals.

Place in a roasting tin with the dripping and roast for 1 hour or until the meat is tender and the skin is brown and crisp. Lift it out, place on a warm serving dish and keep warm.

Pour off most of the fat from the roasting tin, leaving about 2 tbsp of the sediment. Make a thick gravy (see page 59). Serve about 2 slices of meat per person.

Accompaniments: Serve with mint sauce (see page 55) or redcurrant jelly. Cook roast potatoes and parsnips in the oven beside the joint, and serve with buttered cabbage.

Serves 4.

PORK AND BACON

RECIPES

Loin of pork – a classic pork roast (see pages 21 and 24 for roasting instructions). Serve with the traditional accompaniments of roast potatoes, forcemeat balls, apple sauce and gravy (see pages 55-60).

FARMER'S PORK CASSEROLE

Nowadays it is possible to buy boneless slices of shoulder pork, which is reasonable in price and, with slow cooking, has a good flavour. Paprika pepper is a mild, red, powdered pepper, which should always be stored in a dark container as it quickly loses its colour in a bright light.

1½ lb (675g) boneless shoulder pork

---

2 tbsp oil

---

2 medium carrots, sliced

---

2 medium onions, sliced

---

1 small green pepper, seeded and diced

---

8 oz (227g) can of peeled tomatoes

---

1 chicken Oxo cube

½ pt (300ml) water

---

2 level tsp salt

Black pepper

---

3 level tsp paprika pepper

---

2 level tbsp cornflour

---

3 tbsp cold water

Cooking time: About 1½ hours.

Trim any excess fat from the pork. Cut the lean meat into 1 in. (2.5cm) cubes. Heat the oil in a saucepan, add the meat, carrots, onions and green pepper and fry for 3-4 minutes. Add the tomatoes, crumbled Oxo cube, water, salt, freshly ground pepper and paprika pepper and bring to the boil, stirring constantly. Reduce the heat, cover with a lid and simmer gently for 1½ hours or until the pork is tender.

Blend the cornflour with the cold water to a smooth paste and add to the pan, stirring well until the sauce has thickened slightly. Taste and check seasoning. Turn into a warm serving dish.

Accompaniments: Serve with small boiled potatoes and a bright green vegetable, such as peas or broccoli.

Serves 4-6.

SAUSAGE CHUTNEY SLICE

For this recipe, use any chutney that you have in the cupboard. I find it is especially good if you use a dark brown pickle.

---

1 lb (450g) pork sausagemeat

Salt and black pepper

---

1 rounded tbsp chutney

---

1 large cooking apple, peeled, cored and roughly chopped

---

14 oz (397g) packet of puff pastry, thawed

A little beaten egg (to glaze)

Cooking time: About 35 minutes.

Heat the oven to 425°F (220°C) mark 7.

Put the sausagemeat in a bowl with a little freshly ground pepper, salt, chutney and apple and mix together very thoroughly. Shape into a roll 13 in. (32.5cm) long with lightly floured hands.

Roll out the pastry on a lightly floured surface into a rectangle 14 x 11 in. (35 x 27.5cm). Place the sausagemeat down the centre of the pastry and make 6 diagonal cuts through the pastry on either side about 2 in. (5cm) apart to within 1 in. (2.5cm) of the sausagemeat. Brush the edges of the pastry with beaten egg, then alternately cross the pastry strips over the sausagemeat to form a plait. Decorate with pieces of pastry. Brush all over with a little beaten egg and bake in the oven for about 35 minutes or until the pastry is golden brown. Lift it out onto a warm serving dish. Serve with gravy or home-made tomato sauce (see page 55).

Accompaniments: Children like this served with baked beans in tomato sauce. For adults I suggest serving sliced carrots and boiled potatoes.

Serves 4.

Top: Farmer's Pork Casserole.
Bottom: Sausage Chutney Slice.

TRADITIONAL FRENCH COARSE PÂTÉ

Pâtés are not difficult to make. Most good butchers will mince the meat for you, but I suggest that you order it well in advance as some butchers don't always have pig's head and chicken livers in stock. This is a large pâté, which is particularly suitable for a buffet table. I make it either in a large oval terrine or a pâté dish.

1 lb (450g) piece of streaky bacon (the very fatty end part)
1 lb (450g) meat from a pig's head (preferably the fresh pork chap)
1 lb (450g) chicken livers
8 oz (225g) pork sausagemeat
1 onion, quartered
3 cloves of garlic, crushed
6 tbsp sherry
6 oz (175g) fresh white breadcrumbs
4 sprigs of fresh lemon thyme or ½ level tsp dried thyme
1 large egg
1 oz (25g) plain flour
2 level tsp salt
Plenty of black pepper
½ oz (12½g) gelatine
10½ oz (298g) can of condensed consommé
Chopped parsley

Cooking time: About 2 hours.

Heat the oven to 350°F (180°C) mark 4.

Mince the meats, onion and garlic twice. Put the sherry and breadcrumbs in a large bowl and add the leaves from the thyme sprigs. Stir in the minced meat mixture with the egg, flour, salt and freshly ground pepper. Mix thoroughly then turn the mixture into a 4 pt (2.3l) pâté dish or terrine.

Top: Traditional French Coarse Pâté.
Bottom: Family Pâté.

Cover with a lid or foil and stand the pâté dish in a meat tin. Pour hot water into the meat tin until the water comes halfway up the sides of the pâté dish. Cook in the oven for about 2 hours or until the juices run clear when the centre of the pâté is prodded with a fine skewer, yet the very centre remains pink. Remove from the oven, allow to cool, then chill in the refrigerator until cold.

Soak the gelatine in 3 tbsp of cold water in a small bowl, then stand the bowl in a pan of hot water until the gelatine is clear and runny. Remove from the heat and stir in one-quarter of the can of consommé until blended. Add the remaining consommé. Sprinkle the pâté with parsley and pour over the consommé to cover to a depth of about ½ in. (1.25cm) all over the pâté. Chill until set. (There will be some consommé left over, which can be added to soup or used to coat other cold foods.) A lot of gelatine is added to the consommé so that, if the pâté is taken on a picnic and served outside, the jelly will hold up and not melt in the heat. (If making this pâté in winter you could halve the amount of gelatine used.)

Accompaniments: Serve with hot brown bread toast.

Serves 12.

FAMILY PÂTÉ

This is a less expensive pâté than the traditional French one. Again order the meat from the butcher in advance.

1 lb (450g) meat from pig's head cheek (fresh pork chap), minced
1 lb (450g) pig's liver, minced
8 oz (225g) very fatty streaky bacon, minced
1 small onion, finely chopped or minced
2 large cloves of garlic, crushed
2 level tsp salt
Plenty of black pepper
½ level tsp ground nutmeg
1 oz (25g) semolina or ground rice
1 egg, beaten
5 streaky bacon rashers (to line the dish)

Cooking time: About 1¾ hours.

Family Pâté continued from page 126.

Heat the oven to 350°F (180°C) mark 4.

Put all the ingredients except the 5 streaky bacon rashers in a large bowl and mix together very thoroughly. Remove the rind and bone from the 5 rashers of bacon, place on a board and spread flat with the back of a knife. Use the bacon to line the base and sides of a 3 pt (1.7l) dish or terrine, or use a large loaf tin if you have one. Place the meat mixture in the dish and spread flat. Cover the dish with foil, place in a roasting tin half-filled with hot water and cook in the oven for about 1¾ hours. To test if the pâté is cooked, pierce the centre with a skewer: if clear juices run out and the pâté has shrunk slightly from the edges of the dish, it is cooked.

Remove from the oven, allow to become quite cold, then chill in the refrigerator. Turn out onto a serving dish and serve in slices.

Accompaniments: Serve with chunks of French bread.

Serves 8.

SCOTCH EGGS

Dry the eggs thoroughly on kitchen paper, then toss in flour before moulding the sausagemeat around them as this helps to prevent splitting when frying.

1 oz (25g) plain flour
Salt and pepper
4 hard-boiled eggs
1 lb (450g) pork sausagemeat
1 small egg, beaten
Dried breadcrumbs
Oil (for frying)

Cooking time: About 5 minutes.

Put the flour and plenty of salt and pepper in a bag. Shell the eggs and dry them very thoroughly on kitchen paper. Add the eggs to the bag of seasoned flour and shake to coat them thoroughly.

Divide the sausagemeat into 4 equal portions and use to cover each egg, ensuring that there are no cracks in the coating. Brush with beaten egg and coat in the breadcrumbs. Chill in the refrigerator for at least 1 hour before frying.

Heat the oil to 375°F. (If you do not have a thermometer, drop a cube of day-old bread into the oil. If the oil is hot enough, the bread will sink to the bottom, then rise to the surface and brown within 60 seconds.)

Fry the eggs in the oil for about 5 minutes or until they are golden brown all over and the sausagemeat is cooked through. Lift them out, drain thoroughly on kitchen paper and allow to become quite cold.

Accompaniments: Serve with a variety of salads.

Serves 4.

BARBECUED SAUSAGES

Make the baste for these sausages from ingredients that are in your store cupboard. It gives a lovely flavour to a mid-week meal.

1 lb (450g) pork sausages
1-2 tbsp oil
3 tbsp tomato ketchup
2 level tsp made mustard
½ level tsp Worcestershire sauce

Cooking time: About 15 minutes.

Lightly prick the sausages all over and arrange in a single layer in a heatproof dish. Blend together the oil, ketchup, mustard and Worcestershire sauce and spread over the sausages. Leave in a cool place for at least 2 hours, turning occasionally.

Heat the grill to moderate.

Grill the sausages in their dish, basting frequently, for about 15 minutes or until golden brown all over. Serve hot.

Accompaniments: Serve with creamy mashed potatoes and grilled tomatoes or in long bread rolls split in half.

Serves 4.

COURGETTES WITH HAM

This is an inexpensive supper dish which is ideal to make when courgettes are plentiful in the garden. It is always popular in our house, and is an excellent way of using up the end of the bacon joint.

1½ lb (675g) courgettes
2 oz (50g) butter
4 oz (100g) mushrooms, sliced
4-6 oz (100-175g) lean ham, chopped

Sauce
1½ oz (40g) butter
1½ oz (40g) plain flour
¾ pt (450ml) milk
1 chicken Oxo cube
Salt and pepper
3 oz (75g) Cheddar cheese, grated

Cooking time: About 20 minutes.

Wash the courgettes and cut into ¼ in. (0.6cm) slices. Melt the butter in a frying pan and fry the courgettes for 10 minutes, turning occasionally. Add the mushrooms and cook for a further 5 minutes, by which time the courgettes will have turned pale golden brown. Lift them out with a slotted spoon and arrange in a shallow heatproof dish. Cover with the chopped ham.

Meanwhile make the sauce: Melt the butter in a small saucepan, stir in the flour and cook for 2 minutes. Add the milk and bring to the boil, stirring until the sauce has thickened. Add the crumbled Oxo cube and stir until well blended. Taste and check seasoning.

Heat the grill to hot.

Spoon the sauce over the courgettes, sprinkle with the grated cheese and cook under the grill for 3-4 minutes or until the cheese is golden brown and bubbling. Serve immediately.

Accompaniments: This dish is perfect if served with wholemeal bread rolls or chunks of hot French bread.

Serves 4.

GRECIAN PORK

Pork tenderloin, which is sometimes called pork fillet, is always tender and lean. There is no waste, as 1 lb (450g) is plenty for four.

2 tbsp oil
1 lb (450g) pork tenderloin
8 oz (225g) pickling onions
2 cloves of garlic, crushed
½ pt (300ml) inexpensive red wine
1 level tsp salt
Pepper
7½ oz (213g) can of prunes
¾ oz (20g) plain flour
Chopped parsley (to garnish)

Cooking time: About 25 minutes.

Heat the oil in a large frying pan with a lid. Leave the pork in one piece and cook quickly in the hot oil until golden brown. Lift it out and keep on one side. Lower the heat, add the onions and garlic to the pan and cook slowly for about 5 minutes to brown. Pour in the wine and boil quickly for 1 minute to evaporate the alcohol. Lower the heat, return the pork to the pan and season with salt and pepper. Cover with a lid and simmer very slowly for 20 minutes.

Remove the stones from the prunes and blend the prune juice and flour to a smooth paste. Remove the pan from the heat and cut the pork into slices about 1 in. (2.5cm) thick. Blend in the flour and prune juice and stir quickly to make a smooth red sauce.

Add the prunes to the pan, return to the boil and simmer very gently for a further 5 minutes. If the sauce has reduced too much in simmering and is too thick, add a little water to give a light, coating sauce. Taste and check seasoning. Turn the pork into a warm serving dish and sprinkle with parsley.

Accompaniments: Serve with broccoli or French beans and sauté potatoes.

Serves 4.

NORFOLK PORK

This is a rather unusual recipe, which needs to be well seasoned. It is good for an informal supper party, as you can assemble the ingredients and pre-fry them in the morning, then cover and put in the refrigerator at once. The dish then simply needs to be baked in the oven for an hour or so before the meal.

4 lean pork chops
About 1 tbsp seasoned flour
12 oz (350g) onions, chopped
12 oz (350g) Bramley apples, peeled, cored and chopped in chunky pieces
1 tsp salt
Black pepper
½ pt (300ml) cider
Chopped parsley (optional)

Cooking time: About 1 hour.

Remove the rind and excess fat from the pork chops and keep on one side. Put the seasoned flour in a plastic bag, drop in each chop one at a time and shake gently to lightly coat each surface with seasoned flour.

Heat the oven to 350°F (180°C) mark 4.

Place the pieces of excess fat in a large frying pan and heat gently until the bottom of the pan is lightly coated with fat. Lift out these pieces of fat and discard. Add the chops to the pan and brown on both sides. Lift them out onto a plate. Add the onions to the pan and fry gently in the remaining fat for 5 minutes. Add the apples and cook for 3-4 minutes, stirring constantly. Add the salt and plenty of freshly ground pepper.

Place half of the onion and apple mixture in a shallow 2 pt (1l) heatproof dish. Arrange the chops on top, cover with the rest of the onion and apple mixture and pour over the cider. Cook uncovered in the oven for about 1 hour. (If the dish has been prepared in advance and put in the refrigerator, cook in the oven for about 1¼ hours.) Sprinkle with chopped parsley, if used, before serving.

Accompaniments: The thin sauce with this dish is delicious and is good mopped up with creamy mashed potatoes. You could cook small buttered carrots in the oven beside the pork.

Serves 4.

CIDERED COLLAR BACON

Boned collar bacon offers excellent value for money, being a good mixture of lean and fat, and is far cheaper than the gammon cuts. However, it can be a salty joint, so it should be soaked overnight in cold water to remove the excess salt. After boiling, it is simmered until tender. Take care to simmer really slowly as fast cooking tends to shrink and toughen the meat.

3 lb (1.3kg) collar of bacon joint
2 bayleaves
Cider

Glaze
2 level tbsp demerara sugar
2 level tsp dry mustard
2 level tbsp thin honey

Cooking time: About 1 hour 25 minutes.

Use a saucepan of about the same width as the bacon joint. Place the bacon joint in the pan, add the bayleaves and pour over the cider to cover. (If you use a pan of the correct size, you won't have to use too much cider to cover the meat.) Bring to the boil, cover with a lid or foil and simmer very gently for 20 minutes per lb (450g) plus an extra 20 minutes. When the meat is tender, lift it out of the pan, leave until cool enough to handle, then peel off the skin using a small sharp knife. Score the fat in diamond shapes.

Mix together the ingredients for the glaze and spread over the fat. Wrap the lean parts of the bacon in foil, and brown the fat in a very hot oven (450°F [230°C] mark 8) for about 5 minutes or until evenly browned. Serve either hot or cold.

Accompaniments: If you serve this dish hot, it is nice with broad beans or broccoli. Recently I served it with early broad beans from the garden. I cooked them whole in the pod, as with mangetout peas. If you do this, the beans in the pod should be hardly bigger than peas. Cook them in boiling salted water for about 8 minutes, then drain, toss in butter and add freshly ground black pepper.

If you serve this dish cold, French dressed beans and tomatoes are a good accompaniment.

Serves about 10.

Top: Cidered Collar Bacon.
Bottom: Norfolk Pork.

STUFFED PEPPERS WITH CHEESE SAUCE

Cooked rice is just one suggestion for filling the peppers; you could use any left-over cooked meat such as a mixture of chicken and ham. I've also tried fried chicken livers which were very successful. It is essential to season the filling well, so taste it before stuffing the peppers.

4 large even-sized green or red peppers
3 oz (75g) long-grain parboiled rice
1 oz (25g) butter
1 small onion, chopped
4 oz (100g) button mushrooms, sliced
4 streaky bacon rashers, chopped
Salt and black pepper
1 rounded tsp chopped chives
1 egg, beaten
Cheese sauce
1 oz (25g) butter
1 oz (25g) plain flour
½ pt (300ml) milk
1 level tsp made mustard
A little grated nutmeg
Salt and pepper
4 oz (100g) well-flavoured Cheddar cheese, grated

Cooking time: About 45 minutes.

Cut a circle from the base of each green pepper, remove the seeds and keep the circles of flesh and stem on one side. Cook the rice in boiling salted water for 10-12 minutes or until tender, then drain and rinse well. Melt the butter in a frying pan and fry the onion, mushrooms and bacon for 5 minutes. Stir in the cooked rice, salt, plenty of freshly ground pepper and chives. Stir in the egg to bind the rice. Taste and check seasoning.

Heat the oven to 350°F (180°C) mark 4.

Arrange the peppers fairly close together in a heatproof dish and spoon in the filling.

To make the sauce: Melt the butter in a small saucepan, add the flour and cook for 1 minute. Add the milk and bring to the boil, stirring constantly. Simmer until thickened, then add the mustard, nutmeg, salt and pepper. Stir in 2 oz (50g) of the grated cheese.

Pour this sauce around the stuffed peppers. Sprinkle the top of each pepper with the remaining cheese. Cook in the oven for about 45 minutes or until the peppers are tender. Replace the stem 'tops' to decorate, if desired.

Accompaniments: Serve with warm brown bread rolls.

Serves 4.

PARSNIPS AND HAM WITH CHEESE

Use the last cuts of a bacon joint for this recipe. I use 8 oz (225g) of meat, but if you haven't quite enough, simply increase the amount of cheese used to make up this quantity.

A little butter
1 lb (450g) parsnips
8 oz (225g) ham, chopped
8 oz (227g) can of peeled tomatoes
Salt and pepper
2 oz (50g) fresh white breadcrumbs
2 oz (50g) cheese, grated

Cooking time: 40 minutes.

Heat the oven to 350°F (180°C) mark 4.

Butter a 1½ pt (900ml) heatproof dish. Peel the parsnips and cut in quarters lengthwise. Remove the hard centres and cut across into thin slices. Place the parsnips and ham in the dish and pour over the tomatoes. Season well with salt and pepper. Mix together the breadcrumbs and cheese and sprinkle over the top of the dish. Dot with a little butter. Cook in the oven for about 40 minutes or until the parsnips are tender and the breadcrumbs are golden brown and crisp on top. Serve piping hot.

Accompaniments: Serve with slices of French bread.

Serves 4.

Large picture: Stuffed Pepper with Cheese Sauce.
Inset: Parsnips and Ham with Cheese.

BACON AND ONION FLAN

Bake this in a metal flan dish on top of a thick baking sheet so the flan will cook quickly and the base will brown.

Shortcrust pastry
6 oz (175g) plain flour
1½ oz (40g) margarine
1½ oz (40g) lard
About 2 tbsp cold water (for mixing)

Filling
2 oz (50g) butter
8 oz (225g) Spanish onions, thinly sliced
4 oz (100g) streaky bacon, chopped
2 eggs
½ pt (300ml) single cream
Salt and black pepper
2 oz (50g) well-flavoured Cheddar cheese, grated

Cooking time: About 40-45 minutes.

Heat the oven to 425°F (220°C) mark 7.

To make the pastry: Sift the flour into a bowl, cut the margarine and lard into small pieces and rub into the flour with the fingertips until the mixture resembles fine bread-crumbs. Add sufficient water and work in with a knife to make a firm dough. Line a shallow round 9 in. (22.5cm) tin with the pastry and chill in the refrigerator for 10 minutes. Cover with crumpled foil or greaseproof paper and baking beans and bake blind for 15 minutes.

To prepare the filling: Melt the butter in a small saucepan, add the onions and bacon and fry gently for 5 minutes. Remove the flan from the oven and take out the beans and paper. Lift the onion and bacon from the pan with a slotted spoon, drain well and spread over the base of the flan. Blend the eggs with the cream, salt and freshly ground pepper, pour into the flan and sprinkle with cheese.

Reduce the heat to 350°F (180°C) mark 4 and continue cooking for a further 25-30 minutes or until the filling is set and golden brown.

Accompaniments: Serve with a mixed or green salad.

Serves 6.

PORK AND EGG ROLL

This is a good summer recipe. Allow the roll to become quite cold, then chill in the refrigerator and serve sliced for a picnic or packed lunch.

½ oz (12g) plain flour
Salt and pepper
4 hard-boiled eggs
1½ lb (675g) pork sausagemeat
½ level tsp chopped thyme
½ level tsp chopped mixed herbs
2 level tbsp sage and onion stuffing mix

Cooking time: About 30 minutes.

Put the flour and plenty of salt and pepper in a plastic bag. Shell the eggs and dry them very thoroughly on kitchen paper. Put them in the bag with the seasoned flour and shake until well coated.

Mix together the sausagemeat and herbs and add a little extra salt and pepper. Sprinkle a kitchen surface with the sage and onion stuffing mix and roll or pat the sausage-meat into a rectangle 11 x 8 in. (27.5 x 20cm). Arrange the eggs end to end down the centre of the sausagemeat. Firmly wrap over the sausagemeat, pressing well to seal but without stretching it otherwise it will split. Roll the sausagemeat to coat well with the stuffing mix. Lift it onto a baking sheet and chill in the refrigerator for 1 hour.

Heat the oven to 375°F (190°C) mark 5.

Cook the pork and egg roll in the oven for 30 minutes. Remove from the oven, carefully lift it off the baking sheet and place on a flat dish. Allow to cool, then chill in the refrigerator before slicing.

Accompaniments: Serve with a selection of salads.

Serves 4-6.

Top: Bacon and Onion Flan.
Bottom: Pork and Egg Roll.

BRAISED COUNTRY BACON

You could use a vacuum-packed joint for this recipe as it doesn't need to be soaked and takes just a few minutes to get ready for the oven. Alternatively, use a piece of forehock or collar of bacon.

8 oz (225g) carrots, sliced or quartered lengthwise
1 parsnip and/or turnip, chopped
1 large leek, sliced
1½ lb (675g) bacon joint
1 chicken Oxo cube
½ pt (300ml) hot water
4 oz (100g) frozen peas
Salt and pepper

Cooking time: About 1¼ hours.

Heat the oven to 350°F (180°C) mark 4.

Place the carrots, parsnip/turnip and leek in a heatproof casserole and place the bacon on top. Crumble the Oxo cube in the hot water and stir. Pour over the vegetables, lightly cover with a lid or foil and cook in the oven for 1 hour. Remove the foil and stir in the peas. Return to the oven, uncovered, for a further 15 minutes or until the vegetables and bacon are tender. Lift out the bacon and place on a warm serving dish. Taste the vegetables and season if necessary. Serve the vegetables straight from the dish in which they were cooked.

Accompaniments: Serve with plain boiled potatoes.

Serves 6.

Top: Braised Country Bacon.
Bottom: Pork with Red Cabbage.

PORK WITH RED CABBAGE

This is a filling and warming dish for a cold winter's evening. Pork and red cabbage make an excellent combination, and this recipe, using butter beans too, makes a complete meal. Butchers often sell pie pork, which is boneless stewing pork.

6 oz (175g) butter beans
1 lb (450g) pie pork
½ oz (12½g) dripping
2 onions, chopped
1 lb (450g) red cabbage, shredded
1 large cooking apple, peeled, cored and sliced
½ pt (300ml) water
1 level tsp salt
4 cloves
2 tbsp vinegar
1 rounded tbsp moist, dark brown sugar
Fresh chopped parsley (to garnish)

Cooking time: About 1¼ hours.

Put the beans in a bowl, cover with cold water and leave to soak overnight.

The following day, drain off the water. Cut the pork into 1 in. (2.5cm) cubes. Melt the dripping in a large saucepan and fry the pork and onions for 5 minutes. Trim and finely shred the cabbage. Add the butter beans to the pan with the water and bring to the boil. Stir in the cabbage and apple with the salt and cloves. Cover with a tight-fitting lid and cook for about 1¼ hours or until the butter beans and pork are tender. Remove the cloves and stir in the sugar and vinegar. Taste and check seasoning. Turn into a warm serving dish, garnish with chopped parsley and serve very hot.

Serves 4.

PORK 'N' PEACHES

This dish is good enough to serve at a dinner party, and can be made with pork chops, steaks or slices, depending on which is the most attractive or economical buy from your butcher.

15 oz (411g) can of peach halves
2 level tbsp cornflour
¼ level tsp ground ginger
1 tbsp vinegar
1 tbsp soy sauce
1 chicken Oxo cube
4 pork chops, steaks or slices
Butter
1 oz (25g) browned, flaked almonds
½ small green pepper, cut into rings

Cooking time: About 25 minutes.

Drain the peaches and make up the syrup to ½ pt (300ml) with cold water. Place the cornflour in a small saucepan with the ginger, stir in the vinegar, soy sauce, crumbled Oxo cube and peach syrup and bring to the boil, stirring constantly until the sauce has thickened. Simmer for 3 minutes.

Heat the grill to moderate. Trim off any excess fat or rind from the pork. Place the peaches in the bottom of the grill pan, arrange the pork on top of the rack, dot with a little butter and cook for 15-20 minutes or until the pork is tender. Lift out the pork, place on a warm serving dish and arrange the peaches on top. Add the juices from the grill pan to the sauce and heat through. Taste and check seasoning. Spoon the sauce over the pork, sprinkle with the almonds and green pepper rings and serve immediately.

Accompaniments: Serve with a tossed green salad and savoury rice.

Serves 4.

Top: Pork 'n' Peaches.
Bottom: Stuffed Cabbage Leaves.

STUFFED CABBAGE LEAVES

Make this dish in the wintertime when the cabbages are big. Use the large outside leaves for stuffing.

3 oz (75g) long-grain rice
12 large cabbage leaves
12 oz (350g) lean pork
1 medium onion
1 tbsp oil
Salt and pepper
1 egg, beaten
2 level tbsp cornflour
2 tbsp tomato purée
1 chicken Oxo cube
¾ pt (450ml) water

Cooking time: About 45-60 minutes.

Heat the oven to 350°F (180°C) mark 4.

Cook the rice in boiling, salted water as directed on the packet and drain well.

Wash the cabbage leaves thoroughly. Heat a large saucepan of water until boiling, then drop in the leaves, 4 at a time, for about 2 minutes per batch. Lift them out, drain well and trim away the thickest part of the stalk.

Finely mince the pork with the onion. Heat the oil in a frying pan and fry the meat and onion mixture for 5 minutes, stirring constantly. Add the rice and season well with salt and pepper. Remove the pan from the heat and stir in the beaten egg until well mixed.

Divide the meat mixture into 12 equal portions, place a portion in the centre of each cabbage leaf and roll up to form parcels, tucking in the ends. Arrange in a single layer in a shallow heatproof dish.

Place the cornflour, tomato purée, crumbled Oxo cube and water in the frying pan and bring to the boil, stirring until the sauce has thickened. Pour it over the cabbage leaves, cover with a lid or foil and bake in the oven for 45-60 minutes. Serve straight from the dish in which they were cooked.

Accompaniments: Sliced carrots and boiled potatoes.

Serves 4-6.

RAISED PORK PIE

Hot water crust pastry is probably the earliest form of pastry known in England, and is believed to date back to the fourteenth century. I put streaky bacon in this pie as it adds a good flavour and colour.

Hot water crust pastry
12 oz (350g) plain flour
4 oz (100g) lard
1 level tsp salt
¼ pt (150ml) water

Filling
1¼ lb (550g) lean pork
4 oz (100g) streaky bacon, chopped
1 level tsp fresh, chopped sage
1 level tsp salt
1 chicken Oxo cube
¼ pt (150ml) hot water
4 hard-boiled eggs
A little beaten egg (to glaze)
1 level tsp powdered gelatine

Cooking time: About 2½ hours.

To make the pastry: Put the flour in a bowl. Place the lard, salt and water in a saucepan and bring to the boil. Pour immediately onto the flour and mix quickly with a wooden spoon until a smooth dough is formed. Allow to cool until hand-hot but not cold.

To make the filling: Cut the pork into ½ in. (1.25cm) pieces. Put in a bowl with the bacon, sage and salt. Crumble the Oxo cube in the hot water and stir. Add 3 tbsp of this stock to the meat and mix well.

Grease a 7 in. (17.5cm) loose-bottomed cake tin. Take three-quarters of the warm dough (keep the remainder warm) and pat out on a flat surface to a circle 10 in. (25cm) in diameter. Carefully lift this into the tin and draw the dough up the sides to evenly cover the base and sides. Chill in the refrigerator for 5 minutes. Tightly pack half of the meat mixture in the pastry case and place the eggs on top. Cover with the remaining meat. Brush the top edges of the pastry with the beaten egg. Roll out the remaining dough

and cover the pie with it. Press the pastry edges together firmly to seal, and trim off any surplus pastry. (This can be used to make leaves to decorate the top of the pie.) Make a hole in the centre of the pastry lid. Brush with beaten egg and chill in the refrigerator for 10 minutes.

Heat the oven to 425°F (220°C) mark 7.

Cook the pie in the oven for 30 minutes, then reduce the oven temperature to 325°F (160°C) mark 3 and cook for a further 2 hours. If the pastry appears to be getting too brown, cover with a piece of greaseproof paper or foil. Remove from the oven and leave on one side until almost cold.

Sprinkle the gelatine onto the remaining stock and heat gently until dissolved. Pour very carefully down the centre hole made in the pastry lid. Leave in the refrigerator, preferably overnight, until quite cold. When required, remove the tin and place the pie on a serving dish.

Accompaniments: Serve with a selection of salads and buttered new potatoes.

Serves 8.

Raised Pork Pie.

SPICED PORK AND CABBAGE

This delicious dish is made with slices of belly pork and the humble cabbage.

6 slices belly pork
2 oz (50g) butter
2 large onions, sliced
1 clove of garlic, crushed
8 oz (225g) carrots, thinly sliced
1 level tsp mild curry powder
3 tsp soy sauce
½ level tsp salt
1 chicken Oxo cube
4 tbsp water
Black pepper
8 oz (225g) white cabbage, shredded
4 oz (100g) frozen peas

Cooking time: About 30 minutes.

Remove the rind, bones and gristle from the pork slices. Cut the slices in half.

Heat the butter in a saucepan, add the pork and fry gently for 5 minutes, turning once. Add the onions, garlic and carrots and cook for a further 5 minutes, stirring occasionally. Add the curry powder, soy sauce, salt, crumbled Oxo cube, water and freshly ground pepper. Cover with a lid or foil and simmer gently for 20 minutes or until the pork is tender.

Meanwhile cook the cabbage and peas in a little boiling salted water for about 3 minutes or until the cabbage is tender but still very crisp. Drain thoroughly and stir into the pork mixture. Taste and check seasoning. Turn into a warm serving dish and serve immediately.

Serves 4.

WILTSHIRE BACON BAKE

The last pieces of a joint of ham or bacon are often sold quite cheaply at delicatessen counters and are ideal for a dish like this. Left-over cooked potatoes can be used up in this recipe, too.

1 lb (450g) potatoes
8 oz (225g) cooked ham or bacon
6 oz (175g) mushrooms
2 oz (50g) butter
2 oz (50g) plain flour
1 pt (600ml) milk
1 chicken Oxo cube
3 hard-boiled eggs, roughly chopped
Salt and pepper
2 oz (50g) full-flavoured Cheddar cheese, grated
1 oz (25g) Parmesan cheese, grated (optional)

Cooking time: About 25-30 minutes.

Boil the potatoes in their skins until cooked, then drain, peel and slice them. Cut the ham or bacon into neat cubes and slice the mushrooms. Melt the butter in a large saucepan, stir in the flour and cook gently for 2 minutes. Add the milk and crumbled Oxo cube and bring to the boil, stirring until the sauce has thickened.

Heat the grill to hot.

Add the potatoes, bacon, mushrooms and eggs to the sauce, mix well and season with salt and pepper to taste. Turn into a 3 pt (1.7l) heatproof dish and sprinkle with the cheese. Place under the grill and cook until golden brown and hot through.

If the pie has been made in advance, cook it in the oven at 375°F (190°C) mark 5 for 25-30 minutes.

Accompaniments: Serve with French bread and a green salad.

Serves 4-6.

Top: Spiced Pork and Cabbage.
Bottom: Wiltshire Bacon Bake.

PROPER PARTY PIZZA

If you prefer, you could use the ingredients given below to make three or four smaller pizzas – you could freeze one or two after cooking, as they will keep in the freezer for up to a month. Thaw for 1 hour, then cover with foil and reheat in the oven at 350°F (180°C) mark 4 for 20 minutes. If you haven't made bread dough before or have difficulty in obtaining yeast, use a packet of bread mix instead.

Dough

1 lb (450g) strong, plain flour
1 level tsp salt
½ pt (300ml) hand-hot water
2 level tsp dried yeast
1 level tsp sugar
1 tbsp oil

Topping

2-3 tbsp oil
3 large onions, chopped
1-2 cloves of garlic, crushed (optional)
Two 14 oz (397g) cans of peeled tomatoes
8 oz (225g) cooked ham, chopped
8 oz (225g) cheese, grated
Salt and black pepper
2 level tsp dried mixed herbs
Two 1¾ oz (46g) cans of anchovy fillets, drained
12 black olives

Cooking time: About 25-30 minutes.

Sift the flour and salt into a bowl. Pour the hand-hot water into a separate bowl, sprinkle the yeast and sugar into it and allow to stand in a warm place for 10 minutes or until frothy. Make a well in the centre of the flour and stir in the yeast liquid and oil. Mix to a dough, then turn onto a lightly floured surface and knead for 5 minutes to develop the dough. Replace it in the bowl, cover with foil and leave, preferably in a warm place, for about 1 hour or until the dough has doubled in size. (The dough will take longer to double in size if not left in a warm place.)

Meanwhile prepare the filling: Place the oil in a saucepan with the onions and garlic (if used) and fry until soft. Add the tomatoes and cook uncovered until reduced to a thick liquid. Leave to cool. Stir in the ham.

Turn the dough onto a lightly floured surface and press all over to knock out the air. Divide it into 2 pieces and knead each piece into a ball. Roll out to a circle 10 in. (25cm) in diameter and slide onto a greased baking tray. Make a raised rim around the edge of the dough with the knuckles to prevent the filling from falling off.

Spoon the filling over the dough, sprinkle with the cheese, season with salt and freshly ground pepper and sprinkle with dried herbs. Decorate with the anchovy fillets and garnish with the olives. Leave both pizzas to stand in a warm place for about 15 minutes to allow the dough to rise until slightly puffy. Bake in a hot oven (425°F) [220°C] mark 7) for 25-30 minutes or until the edges of the dough are pale golden brown.

A large pizza serves 4.

Proper Party Pizzas.

KENTUCKY CHOPS

The sauce in this recipe uses ingredients which are likely to be in your store cupboard. The dish is quickly assembled, and the sauce gives the chops a nice glaze.

4 lean pork chops
4 level tbsp clear honey
2 tbsp soy sauce
1 tbsp tomato ketchup
1 tbsp wine vinegar
1 level tbsp tomato purée
Salt and pepper
A few drops of Tabasco sauce
Juice of 1 small orange
8 oz (225g) patna rice
Small sprigs of watercress (to garnish)

Cooking time: About 40 minutes.

Heat the oven to 375°F (190°C) mark 5.

Remove any excess fat from the chops. Place the chops in a shallow heatproof dish. Blend together all the ingredients, except the rice, in a bowl, then pour over the chops. Bake uncovered in the oven for about 40 minutes, basting occasionally, until the chops are tender.

Meanwhile cook the rice in plenty of fast boiling, salted water for about 12 minutes or as directed on the packet. Drain very well and turn onto a serving dish. Arrange the chops on top and spoon over any sauce. Garnish with small sprigs of watercress.

Accompaniments: Serve with crisp green salad.

Serves 4.

Top: Kentucky Chops.
Bottom: Pork Hongroise.

PORK HONGROISE

If you have difficulty in obtaining soured cream for this recipe, buy double cream instead and sour it by adding 2 tbsp lemon juice.

1½ lb (675g) pork fillet or boned loin of pork
2 tbsp oil
1 oz (25g) butter
1 onion, chopped
1 level tbsp paprika pepper
½ oz (12½g) plain flour
½ pt (300ml) water
1 chicken Oxo cube
5 tbsp sherry
1 level tsp tomato purée
Salt and pepper
6 oz (175g) small button mushrooms
½ oz (12½g) cornflour
2 tbsp cold water
¼ pt (150ml) carton of soured cream

Cooking time: About 40 minutes.

Cut the pork into 1½ in. (3.5cm) pieces. Heat the oil in a saucepan, add the butter and quickly fry the pork pieces until they are just beginning to brown. Remove them from the pan and drain on kitchen paper.

Add the onion and paprika pepper to the pan and fry for 2 minutes. Remove the pan from the heat, blend in the flour and cook for 1 minute. Stir in the water, crumbled Oxo cube, sherry and tomato purée, return to the heat and bring to the boil, stirring constantly until the sauce has thickened. Season well with salt and pepper and add the meat. Cover with a lid or foil and simmer for about 40 minutes or until the pork is tender.

At the end of the cooking time, add the whole mushrooms. Blend the cornflour to a smooth paste with the water, add to the pan and bring to the boil. Just before serving, stir in the soured cream or turn into a warm serving dish and spoon the soured cream on top. Serve immediately.

Accompaniments: Noodles and a green salad.

Serves 4-6.

ROLLED HAND OF PORK

As this is one of the cheapest, slightly coarse cuts of pork, roast it first in a hot oven, then reduce the temperature and cook it more slowly. This will give you a very tender joint.

Stuffing

1 small onion, chopped
1 stick of celery, chopped
1 oz (25g) butter
1 large cooking apple, peeled, cored and chopped
3 oz (75g) fresh white or brown breadcrumbs
1 level tbsp fresh, chopped sage
1 egg, beaten
Salt and pepper

1 hand of pork, boned
Salt and pepper
Oil
Coarse salt

Cooking time: About 3½-3¾ hours.

Heat the oven to 400°F (200°C) mark 6.

To prepare the stuffing: Place the onion, celery and butter in a small saucepan and cook gently for 10 minutes. Add the apple and cook for a further 2 minutes. Remove the pan from the heat and stir in the breadcrumbs, sage, beaten egg, salt and pepper.

Open the pork flat and season lightly with salt and pepper. Put the stuffing in the pocket of the joint, press the pork back into shape and secure with fine skewers.

Weigh the joint. Rub the skin with the oil and coarse salt to ensure a crisp crackling. Put the meat on a rack in a roasting tin and roast in the oven for 45 minutes.

Reduce the oven temperature to 325°F (160°C) mark 3 and roast for a further 30 minutes to the lb (450g) plus an extra 30 minutes. Lift out the pork and place on a warm serving dish. Make a gravy from the juices in the roasting tin (see page 58).

Accompaniments: Serve with apple sauce (see page 58) and with braised celery or carrots.

Serves at least 12.

BUCKS BACON BADGER

A sort of savoury roly-poly pudding, this recipe was given to me by a lady in our village who remembers her great-grandmother making it.

Filling

8-10 oz (225-275g) bacon pieces
1 onion, finely chopped
1 potato, finely diced

Pastry

8 oz (225g) self-raising flour
4 oz (100g) shredded suet
½ level tsp salt
1 tbsp chopped parsley
About 8 tbsp cold water

Cooking time: About 1 hour.

Heat the oven to 400°F (200°C) mark 6.

Remove the rind and bone from the bacon and cut the lean meat into small pieces. Put them in a bowl, add the onion and potato and mix well.

To make the pastry: Put the flour, suet, salt and parsley in a bowl and mix to a soft but not sticky dough with the water. Roll out on a lightly floured surface to a rectangle 15 x 12 in. (37.5 x 30cm). Brush the edges with water.

Spread the filling over the pastry to within 1 in. (2.5cm) of the edges. Loosely roll up the pastry like a Swiss roll and seal the ends firmly. Lift onto a piece of greased foil and cover loosely. Place on a baking sheet and bake in the oven for 45 minutes.

Open the foil and cook for a further 15 minutes to allow the top to brown. Cut in slices and serve hot.

Accompaniments: Tomato sauce or a rich onion gravy (see pages 55 and 59) go well with this dish. Serve with cabbage and buttered carrots.

Serves 4.

Top: Rolled Hand of Pork.
Bottom: Bucks Bacon Badger.

OLD-FASHIONED COOKED HAM

To be technically correct – which I am not in this case – a ham isn't called ham until it is cooked; until then, it is known as gammon. However, the York variety is known as ham even in the uncooked state. I consider raw York ham to be one of the best available; being a dry salt cure it has a fine flavour and is less salty than some others. Order it from your butcher well in advance, and ask him to saw off the last 2-3 in. (5-7.5cm) from the knuckle end bone. The ham will then fit into the pan more easily.

In the past, I have used recipes for cooking a ham which involved bringing it to the boil and simmering very gently for about 3 hours. However, I always found that this method would shrink the ham and somewhat overcook it. Having tried an updated version of the haybox instead, I have found that the result is superb and very easy to do.

You will need a very large pan in which to cook the ham. I use an oval 'dixie' which I bought at a jumble sale, but you could try borrowing something suitable from a local school or club if you don't have one large enough.

---

1 York ham (14-16 lb [6.3-7.2kg] in weight)

Glaze

About 4 oz (100g) demerara sugar

---

1 tbsp dry English mustard

Cooking time: About 21¾ hours.

Remove any wrappings from the ham and wash off any mould. (This bloom is not harmful; it simply shows that the ham is mature, like a good cheese.) Soak the ham in cold water for 48 hours, then drain off the water.

Place the ham in the large saucepan, cover with cold water and a lid. Bring to the boil, then simmer very gently for 1½ hours. At the end of the cooking time, bring to the boil again and place in your haybox immediately.

To make the haybox: In an undisturbed corner of the kitchen, place a couple of old blankets on the floor, open out a quilted sleeping bag or duvet on top, followed by opened newspapers. Place the saucepan in the centre, fold over the newspapers, then the sleeping bag or duvet and finally the blankets, so that the pan is completely wrapped up in a cocoon. Do not disturb, or else the pan will lose heat. Leave overnight or for 20 hours.

The following day, you will find that the pan is still hot. Lift out the ham and ease off the skin using a small palette knife. Score a diagonal pattern on the fat using a sharp knife, taking care not to cut through as far as the lean ham.

Heat the oven to 425°F (220°C) mark 7.

Mix together the sugar and mustard and pat over the fat surface of the ham. Lift the ham into a roasting tin and cook in the oven for 5-15 minutes, turning it until it is evenly browned all over. Leave to become cold.

For a 5-10 lb (2.3-4.5kg) gammon, prepare as detailed in the method above, but cook for 1 hour only before leaving in the haybox overnight. Ask your butcher about the soaking time required for the joint, as gammons vary in saltiness and will only need to be soaked overnight instead of for 48 hours.

Accompaniments: Serve with mustard or Cumberland sauce (see page 58).

Serves at least 20.

Old-fashioned Cooked Ham.

JUGGED PORK

This is a delicious pork casserole that is full of flavour. If you serve it with forcemeat balls it is good enough for a special supper or dinner.

1¼ lb (550g) lean pork
1 oz (25g) bacon fat
1 large onion, sliced
2 cloves
1 bayleaf
¼ pt (150ml) water
1 chicken Oxo cube
¼ pt (150ml) inexpensive red wine
Salt and black pepper

Forcemeat balls
2 oz (50g) fresh white breadcrumbs
1 level tsp fresh, chopped sage
1 oz (25g) shredded suet
Salt and pepper
A little beaten egg

Cooking time: About 1 hour.

Cut the meat into 1 in. (2.5cm) cubes. Place the bacon fat in a saucepan and fry the pork with the onion for 3-4 minutes. Add the cloves and bayleaf (for ease, stick the cloves into the bayleaf) with the water, crumbled Oxo cube, wine, salt and freshly ground pepper and bring to the boil. Cover with a lid or foil and simmer gently for about 1 hour or until the pork is tender.

Meanwhile put the breadcrumbs in a bowl with the sage and suet, season well with salt and pepper and add sufficient beaten egg to bind the mixture together. Mix well. Shape into 8 balls and fry in a little hot oil for 4-5 minutes, turning constantly until golden brown all over. Remove from the pan and drain on kitchen paper.

Taste the pork and check seasoning. Remove the bayleaf and cloves. Turn into a warm serving dish and arrange the forcemeat balls around the edge of the dish.

Accompaniments: This dish is nice if served with creamy mashed potatoes to absorb the gravy, and a green vegetable such as broccoli or French beans.

Serves 4.

CALIFORNIAN PORK

This is a rather special way of serving pork which is ideal for a dinner party. If you have any inexpensive brandy left over from a holiday abroad, soak the prunes in it; if not, increase the amount of red wine used by 6 tbsp.

4 lb (1.8kg) boned shoulder of pork
1 large onion, sliced
½ pt (300ml) inexpensive red wine
2 bayleaves
About 6 peppercorns
12 prunes
6 tbsp inexpensive brandy or red wine

Beurre manié
1½ oz (40g) butter
1½ oz (40g) plain flour
Salt and pepper

Cooking time: About 2¼ hours.

If the butcher has tied the pork, remove the string and place the pork flat in a casserole with the onion, wine, bayleaves and peppercorns. Cover and allow to marinate overnight.

Stone the prunes and put in a small bowl with the brandy or wine. Allow to soak overnight so that all the brandy or wine is absorbed.

The following day, heat the oven to 450°F (230°C) mark 8.

Lift the pork from the marinade and pack the prunes into the cavities of the meat. Roll it up and tie securely with string. Put the meat in a roasting tin and pour over the

Top: Californian Pork.
Bottom: Jugged Pork.

Californian Pork continued from page 152.

strained marinade. Roast the pork in the oven for 15 minutes, then reduce the oven temperature to 350°F (180°C) mark 4 and cook for a further 2 hours, basting occasionally.

Lift out the pork, place on a warm serving dish and keep warm. Cream the butter with the flour to make a smooth paste. Gradually add to the juices in the roasting tin, whisking well until all the butter and flour paste has been added. Bring to the boil, stirring until the sauce has thickened. Taste and check seasoning. Simmer for 2 minutes. Pour the sauce into a sauce boat and serve with the pork.

Accompaniments: Serve with roast potatoes, parsnips and Brussels sprouts.

Serves 12.

MARJORAM PORK CHOPS

Marjoram is such an easy herb to grow and is a perennial plant. It is used far more often in European countries; in Italy it grows wild and is called oregano. It is better to use fresh rather than dried marjoram, and it is especially good with tomato dishes such as this one.

4 pork chops
2 large onions, sliced
2 cloves of garlic, crushed
14 oz (397g) can of peeled tomatoes
1 level tbsp fresh, chopped marjoram
Salt and pepper
2 tbsp vinegar
2 level tbsp dark brown sugar

Cooking time: About 45-60 minutes.

Heat the oven to 350°F (180°C) mark 4.

Remove the rind and excess fat from the pork chops. Place the fat in a large frying pan and heat gently until the base of the pan is lightly coated with fat. Lift out these pieces of fat

with a slotted spoon and discard. Add the chops to the pan and fry for 3-4 minutes until browned on both sides. Lift them out and arrange in a single layer in a heatproof dish.

Add the onions and garlic to the pan and fry gently for 2-3 minutes. Stir in the tomatoes, marjoram, salt, pepper, vinegar and sugar and bring to the boil, stirring constantly. Pour over the chops and bake uncovered in the oven for about 45 minutes or until the chops are tender. If the chops are thick, allow a further 5-10 minutes' cooking time. Taste and check seasoning. Serve straight from the dish in which it was cooked.

Accompaniments: Serve with plain ribbon noodles and a tossed green salad.

Serves 4.

SAUSAGE POMODORIAN

If you grow your own tomatoes, this recipe is a very good way of using up all those small tomatoes that never seem to grow quite big enough to serve.

1 lb (450g) tomatoes
4 streaky bacon rashers
1 lb (450g) chipolata sausages
1 clove of garlic, crushed
1 level tsp castor sugar
Salt and pepper
1 bayleaf

Cooking time: 10 minutes.

Put the tomatoes in a bowl, cover with boiling water and leave for about 10 seconds, then drain. Peel off the skins and roughly chop the tomatoes. Remove the rind and bone from the bacon and cut it into thin strips. Place the bacon and sausages in a frying pan and fry quickly to brown on all sides, turning frequently. Add the garlic, tomatoes, sugar, salt, pepper and bayleaf, reduce the heat and cook gently for about 8 minutes. Turn onto a hot serving dish. Remove the bayleaf.

Accompaniments: This dish is delicious served with courgettes or peas and sauté potatoes.

Serves 4.

KIDNEY STUFFED PORK CHOPS

Pig's kidney is often one of the more inexpensive kidneys and really adds flavour to the stuffing. Before dicing the kidney, snip the skin and peel it off, then remove the core with scissors.

4 loin pork chops
1 pig's kidney
1 onion
1 oz (25g) butter
½ oz (12½g) fresh brown breadcrumbs
½ tsp thyme
½ level tsp salt
Black pepper

Sauce
3 tomatoes
1 rounded tsp plain flour
¼ pt (150ml) water
1 rounded tsp tomato purée
2 tsp Worcestershire sauce
½ tsp salt
Pepper

Cooking time: About 20 minutes.

Trim the excess fat from the chops and remove the rind. Insert the tip of a sharp knife into the fat side of the chop and cut inwards to make a large pocket in the meat. Finely dice the kidney, discarding the core, and chop the onion finely. Melt the butter in a saucepan, add the kidney and onion and cook quickly for about 5 minutes or until golden brown.

Heat the grill to moderate.

Remove the pan from the heat and stir in the breadcrumbs, thyme, salt and freshly ground pepper. Cool the stuffing, divide into 4 portions and use a teaspoon to fill the chops with it. Press to flatten slightly without loosening the stuffing.

Cook the chops under the grill for about 10 minutes on each side. Remove and keep warm on a serving dish. Meanwhile peel and cut the tomatoes into wedges. Pour the sediment and juices from the grill pan into a small saucepan. Blend in the flour, stir in the water and bring to the boil. Add the tomatoes, tomato purée, Worcestershire sauce, salt and pepper, cook for 1 minute, then pour over the meat. Serve immediately.

Accompaniments: Serve with sauté potatoes and a mixed green salad or broccoli.

Serves 4.

BACON AND EGG TORTILLA PAN FRY

For this recipe it is best to use a non-stick frying pan, as it makes serving much easier. This is a great favourite in our household for a light lunch or supper dish, and the children think that it is great fun to make it themselves.

6 streaky bacon rashers
2 level tbsp plain flour
6 tbsp milk
4 eggs
Salt and black pepper
2 tomatoes, sliced

Cooking time: About 10 minutes.

Remove the rind and bone from the bacon rashers and place in a 9 in. (22.5cm) non-stick frying pan. Cook gently until the fat has run out and the bacon is golden brown and crisp. Lift it out and keep warm.

Meanwhile blend together the flour and milk and beat in the eggs, salt and freshly ground pepper. Pour the egg mixture into the bacon fat remaining in the pan and cook over moderate heat until set, tilting the pan slightly to let the egg mixture run underneath occasionally, but do not stir. Arrange the cooked rashers on top of the egg tortilla. Garnish with tomato slices. Serve straight from the pan.

Accompaniments: Serve with bread rolls or slices of French bread.

Serves 3.

BOSTON BAKED BEANS

This dish benefits from being cooked slowly. It is not essential to soak the beans overnight, but it is far better if you do so. If you do not have time to soak the beans, increase the cooking time by a further 2 hours and add a little extra stock.

12 oz (350g) haricot beans
1½ pt (900ml) water
2 chicken Oxo cubes
1 tbsp black treacle
1 tbsp golden syrup
2 tbsp soft, dark brown sugar
2 level tsp dry mustard
2 level tbsp tomato purée
2 level tsp salt
Black pepper
8 oz (225g) salt belly pork or an unsmoked piece of bacon
2 large onions

Cooking time: About 4-6 hours.

Wash the beans, put in a bowl, cover with cold water and leave to soak overnight.

The following day, drain off the water and discard. Place the beans in a saucepan with the 1½ pt (900ml) of water and crumbled Oxo cubes. Bring to the boil, then simmer for 30 minutes.

Heat the oven to 275°F (140°C) mark 2.

Take a large 4½ pt (2.5l) heatproof casserole and put in the treacle, syrup, sugar, mustard, tomato purée, salt and freshly ground pepper and stir until well blended. Remove the skin from the pork or bacon and cut into ½ in. (1.25cm) cubes, cut the onions into wedges and add the meat and onions to the casserole. Remove the beans from the heat, add with their cooking liquor to the casserole and stir well. Cover with a lid and cook in the oven for 4-6 hours, stirring occasionally.

If the dish is too liquid, remove the lid towards the end of the cooking time for about 30 minutes. If too dry, add a little extra water.

Accompaniments: Serve this dish with garlic bread.

Serves 4-6.

AMERICAN SPARE RIBS

These ribs in their piquant, sticky sauce are messy to eat and are therefore best tackled with the fingers and large paper napkins. It is a very good dish to eat out of doors on a sunny day.

2 tbsp oil
12 oz (350g) onions, chopped
2 cloves of garlic, crushed
4 tbsp vinegar
2½ oz (62g) can of tomato purée
¼ tsp chilli powder
6 tbsp clear honey
2 red Oxo cubes, crumbled
½ pt (300ml) water
2½ lb (1.1kg) pork ribs
Salt and black pepper

Cooking time: About 1 hour.

Heat the oven to 375°F (190°C) mark 5.

Heat the oil in a large saucepan, add the onions and fry gently for about 15 minutes or until pale golden brown and soft. Add all the remaining ingredients except the ribs and bring to the boil, stirring constantly. Simmer uncovered for 10 minutes.

Arrange the ribs in a single layer in a shallow heatproof dish, season with salt and freshly ground pepper and pour over half the sauce. Cook in the oven for 45 minutes. Remove from the oven and drain off the surplus fat or oil or blot with kitchen paper. Coat with the remaining sauce and roast for a further 15-30 minutes or until golden brown and tender.

Accompaniments: Serve with a crisp green salad and warm bread rolls.

Serves 4.

Top: Boston Baked Beans.
Bottom: American Spare Ribs.

BUTTER BEAN AND BACON CASSEROLE

Smoked forehock has a rich flavour, so if you prefer a milder taste, use a green, unsmoked joint which often does not need to be soaked. Ask your butcher whether he recommends you to soak the particular joint you buy.

1½-2 lb (675-900g) smoked forehock of bacon
8 oz (225g) butter beans
2 pt (1-1l) boiling water
2 medium onions, sliced
2 carrots, sliced in rings
Black pepper
¾ pt (450ml) cider
Plenty of fresh, chopped parsley

Cooking time: About 4 hours.

Soak the bacon joint in cold water overnight. Put the butter beans in a large bowl, cover with the boiling water and soak overnight.

The following day, strain off all the water. Put the beans, onions and carrots in a 4 pt (2.3l) heatproof casserole. Season with freshly ground pepper and pour over the cider. Arrange the bacon joint on top, cover with a lid or foil and cook in the oven at 300°F (150°C) mark 2 for about 4 hours or until the bacon is very tender.

Remove the dish from the oven, lift out the joint, recover the dish and keep it hot. With a sharp knife, remove all the skin from the bacon (it helps to have a carving fork in your other hand), cut the meat off the bone, then slice it into bite-sized pieces. Add the meat to the beans and vegetables, stir lightly and taste to see if it is salty enough. Sprinkle with plenty of chopped parsley.

Accompaniments: Serve with a crunchy salad of shredded red and white cabbage, celery, chopped nuts, green pepper and cucumber, tossed in French dressing.

Serves 4.

GAMMON AND MUSTARD SAUCE

Try serving gammon with this sauce to make a change from the usual pineapple slices.

2 oz (50g) soft, light brown sugar
1 oz (25g) plain flour
2 level tsp dry mustard
Salt and pepper
½ pt (300ml) water
1 chicken Oxo cube
4 tbsp white wine vinegar
4 gammon steaks
2 oz (50g) butter
Small sprigs of watercress (to garnish)

Cooking time: About 10 minutes.

Place the sugar, flour, mustard, salt and pepper in a small saucepan. Add half of the water, a little at a time, stirring constantly until blended to a smooth paste. Add the remaining water with the crumbled Oxo cube and vinegar. Bring to the boil over moderate heat, stirring constantly until the sauce has thickened. Reduce the heat and simmer for 10 minutes.

Meanwhile heat the grill to moderate.

Place the gammon steaks in the grill pan and dot with butter. Grill the steaks for 5 minutes on each side. Lift them out and arrange on a warm serving dish. Stir any juices from the grill pan into the sauce. Taste and check seasoning. Garnish the steaks with small sprigs of watercress. Serve the sauce separately.

Accompaniments: Serve with sauté potatoes, peas and grilled, halved tomatoes.

Serves 4.

POULTRY

RECIPES

Classic roast turkey (see pages 31-32 for roasting
instructions). Serve with the traditional accompaniments of
bacon rolls, sausages, bread sauce and gravy
(see pages 55-60).

DUCK À L'ORANGE

For four people, you will need a duck weighing about 5 lb (2.3kg); for eight, buy two ducks. If preferred, the duck may be carved before going to the table. Place the pieces in a roasting tin and reheat in the oven for about 10 minutes.

5 lb (2.3kg) duck
A little butter
Salt and black pepper

Orange sauce
2 tbsp duck fat
1 oz (25g) plain flour
4 fl oz (100ml) port
½ pt (300ml) giblet stock
2 large oranges
1 tbsp redcurrant jelly

Watercress (to garnish)

Cooking time: About 2 hours.

Heat the oven to 400°F (200°C) mark 6.

Remove the giblets from the duck and put them in a heat-proof casserole with a little onion, freshly ground pepper and about ¾ pt (450ml) water. Cover with a lid or foil and put in the bottom of the oven.

Prick the duck all over with a sharp-pronged fork. Rub with a very small amount of butter and season well with salt and freshly ground pepper. Place on a rack or trivet in a roasting tin. Roast without basting for 1¾-2 hours or until the duck is tender. Remove the duck from the oven and pour any juices inside it into a measuring jug. Skim off all the fat from the roasting tin, add any remaining juices in the pan to the jug and keep the fat on one side. Place the duck on a warm serving dish and keep warm.

Place 2 tbsp of duck fat in a small saucepan, add the flour and cook gently until pale golden brown. Remove the pan from the heat and slowly add the port. Make up the duck juices in the measuring jug to ½ pt (300ml) with stock from the giblets and add to the pan. Return the pan to the heat and bring to the boil, stirring until the sauce has thickened. Season with salt and pepper and simmer gently for 5 minutes to allow the sauce to reduce slightly.

Thinly peel one orange (removing the zest only), shred finely, simmer for 3 minutes in a little water, then drain well. Squeeze the juice from one and a half oranges and cut the remaining half in thin slices for garnish. Add the orange juice and redcurrant jelly to the pan and stir constantly until the jelly has dissolved. Taste and check seasoning. Sprinkle the duck with the orange rind and garnish with orange slices and watercress. Serve the sauce separately.

Accompaniments: Serve with garden peas and creamed or new potatoes.

Serves 4.

Duck à l'Orange.

ANNIVERSARY TURKEY

This is one of the best ways of serving cooked turkey. It is an ideal party dish as it is best made the day before it is needed to allow the flavours to blend.

1 small onion, chopped
A little butter
½ clove of garlic, crushed
1 tbsp tomato purée
½ level tsp curry powder
2 tbsp lemon juice
2 tbsp apricot jam
1 chicken Oxo cube
¼-½ pt (150-300ml) good mayonnaise
¾-1 lb (350-450g) cooked turkey, chopped
8 oz (225g) green and black grapes, halved and stoned
1½ oz (40g) browned, flaked almonds
Small sprigs of watercress or parsley or lettuce (to garnish)

Gently sauté the onion in butter with the garlic for 5 minutes or until soft. Add the tomato purée, curry powder, 1 tbsp of lemon juice, apricot jam and crumbled Oxo cube. Heat gently until the jam has melted, then purée in a blender or sieve into a small bowl. Allow to cool, then stir into the mayonnaise and fold in the turkey. Cover and chill in the refrigerator overnight.

The following day, toss the grapes in the remaining lemon juice and stir into the turkey mayonnaise. Taste and check seasoning. Turn into a serving dish and sprinkle with the almonds. Garnish with small sprigs of watercress, parsley or lettuce.

Accompaniments: Serve with slices of French bread and an assortment of salads.

Serves 6.

ROBOROUGH TURKEY

This is a good way to serve left-over turkey.

2 oz (50g) butter
2 oz (50g) plain flour
3 level tsp mild curry powder
¾ pt (450ml) water
2 chicken Oxo cubes
2 level tsp soft, dark brown sugar
Salt and pepper
14 oz (397g) can of peeled tomatoes
1¼ lb (550g) cooked turkey pieces
12 oz (340g) can of sweetcorn kernels, drained
10 oz (280g) can of asparagus pieces or tips, drained

Cooking time: About 20 minutes.

Melt the butter in a large saucepan, add the flour and curry powder and cook for 2 minutes. Stir in the water, crumbled Oxo cubes and sugar and bring to the boil, stirring until the sauce has thickened. Season with salt and pepper and add the tomatoes. Cover with a lid and simmer gently for 15 minutes.

Add the turkey, sweetcorn and asparagus to the sauce and reheat for 5 minutes. Taste and check seasoning. Turn into a warm casserole and serve piping hot.

Accompaniments: Serve this dish with a large bowl of plain boiled rice, and possibly a green salad or some garden peas.

Serves 6.

Top: Anniversary Turkey.
Bottom: Roborough Turkey.

TURKEY SEVILLANA

Carefully brown the turkey rolls on all sides when frying, as this gives a nutty flavour and adds colour to the dish. The browning should not be done too quickly as a very fierce heat can make the rolls too dark.

4 oz (100g) butter
1 onion, chopped
4 oz (100g) mushrooms, chopped
2 oz (50g) stuffed green olives
2 oz (50g) fresh white breadcrumbs
1 egg, beaten
Salt and pepper
4 pieces of turkey breast fillets (each about 5-6 oz [150-175g] in weight)
1½ oz (40g) plain flour
¼ pt (150ml) water
1 chicken Oxo cube
1 orange
1 tbsp sherry
¼ pt (150ml) single cream

Cooking time: About 20 minutes.

Melt 2 oz (50g) of butter in a saucepan, add the onion and fry for about 5 minutes or until cooked but not brown. Add the mushrooms and cook for a further 2 minutes. Chop 1 oz (25g) of olives and add to the pan with the bread-crumbs and egg, add salt and pepper to taste and mix together well. Divide the mixture between the turkey pieces, spread flat then roll up and secure with string or wooden cocktail sticks.

Melt the remaining butter in a frying pan and fry the rolls until golden brown, turning regularly until cooked through. Lift them out and arrange on a warm serving dish. Remove the string or cocktail sticks.

Turkey Sevillana.

Stir the flour into the fat remaining in the pan and slowly add the water and crumbled Oxo cube and bring to the boil, stirring until thickened. Cut thin strips of the orange rind for garnish, squeeze the juice from the orange and add to the pan with the sherry and cream. Bring to the boil, stirring constantly. Season to taste. Pour some sauce over the rolls and serve the remainder in a sauce boat. Garnish with the remaining olives and sprinkle strips of orange rind on top.

Accompaniments: Duchesse potatoes and French beans.

Serves 4.

HURRY SCURRY CHICKEN

An easy, almost instant sort of casserole. There is no need to fry the joints: just remove the skin. You could use a can of mushrooms if you haven't any fresh ones. This dish is good enough to serve for a quickly prepared supper with friends.

4 chicken portions
Salt and black pepper
1-2 level tsp paprika pepper
4 oz (100g) button mushrooms
10½ oz (298g) can of condensed mushroom soup
¼ pt (150ml) double cream
A little chopped parsley and chives, mixed

Cooking time: About 1 hour.

Heat the oven to 350°F (180°C) mark 4.

Remove the skin from the chicken and trim off any pieces of fat and spare bits of bone. Place the pieces in a single layer in a heatproof dish and season with salt and freshly ground pepper. Sprinkle with the paprika pepper and add the mushrooms. Put the soup in a small bowl and stir in the cream until thoroughly blended. Pour over the chicken and bake uncovered in the oven for 1 hour or until tender. Remove from the oven, sprinkle with the chopped parsley and chives and serve immediately.

Accompaniments: This dish is lovely served with courgettes and sauté potatoes.

Serves 4.

GRILLED HERBED CHICKEN

This recipe can easily be adapted to cater for a crowd or a quick supper for two. It is an excellent recipe to serve on a warm summer evening – especially when cooked on a barbecue.

6 oz (175g) butter
2 cloves of garlic, crushed
Salt and black pepper
2 level tbsp fresh, chopped parsley
2 level tbsp fresh, chopped mixed herbs
6 chicken portions

Cooking time: 25-30 minutes.

Remove the rack from the grill pan and heat the grill to moderate.

Put the butter in a bowl with the garlic, salt, freshly ground pepper and herbs and cream thoroughly until well blended. Place the chicken portions (skin side uppermost) in the grill pan, spread with half of the garlic and herb butter and cook under the grill for 15 minutes, basting occasionally.

Turn the chicken over and spread with the remaining butter, replace under the grill and continue cooking for a further 10-15 minutes or until the chicken is golden brown and tender. The cooking time will vary slightly with the size of the chicken portions (legs take longer to cook through than wings). To test if the chicken is cooked, prick with a sharp pointed knife: if clear juices run out, it is cooked. Lift the chicken onto a serving dish and spoon over the juices from the pan.

Accompaniments: New potatoes and a green or mixed salad go very well with this dish.

Serves 6.

Top: Chicken Gougère.
Bottom: Grilled Herbed Chicken.

CHICKEN GOUGÈRE

This is a savoury filling baked inside the same choux paste that is used to make chocolate éclairs. You can change the filling according to the ingredients in your larder: ham is very good in this sauce – add a teaspoonful of good mustard for an extra-special dish.

Choux paste
4 oz (100g) butter
½ pt (300ml) water
5 oz (150g) plain flour
4 eggs
½ level tsp salt
Pepper

Filling
1 onion, finely chopped
1½ oz (40g) butter
2 level tsp paprika pepper
1 oz (25g) plain flour
1 chicken Oxo cube
½ pt (300ml) hot water
6 oz (175g) button mushrooms, sliced
8 oz (225g) cooked chicken, diced
Chopped parsley (to garnish)

Cooking time: About 35-45 minutes.

To prepare the choux paste: Place the butter and water in a saucepan and bring slowly to the boil to allow the butter to melt. Remove the pan from the heat. Sprinkle the flour into the mixture and stir vigorously with a wooden spoon to make a thick paste which will cling to the spoon and leave the pan clean. Allow to cool slightly.

To prepare the filling: Cook the onion in the butter for about 10 minutes or until soft but not coloured. Add the paprika pepper and flour and cook gently for 1 minute. Crumble the Oxo cube in the hot water, stir and add to the pan. Bring to the boil, stirring constantly. Add the mushrooms and simmer for 5 minutes. Stir in the chicken and allow to cool. Taste and check seasoning.

Chicken Gougère continued from page 167.

To complete the choux paste: Whisk the eggs and gradually beat into the pan, one spoonful at a time. When all the egg has been added, the mixture will be stiff enough to hold its shape. Beat in the salt and pepper.

Heat the oven to 400°F (200°C) mark 6.

Grease the base and sides of a 3 pt (1.7l) shallow heatproof dish. Spoon the choux paste around the edge of the dish to form an even border and then place the filling in the centre. Bake in the oven for 35-45 minutes or until the paste is well risen and golden brown. Garnish with chopped parsley. Serve immediately.

Accompaniments: A green vegetable such as broccoli or green beans is perfect with this dish.

Serves 4-6.

SPANISH PAELLA

This is a real party dish which is by no means cheap to make but is well worth it for a special occasion. I have found it best to finish cooking this dish in the oven to avoid constant stirring, although in Spain it is cooked on the hob throughout. Paella is traditionally cooked in a round pan with two handles called a *paellera*, but at home I use either an old frying pan with short metal handles or a shallow heatproof dish.

6 tbsp salad oil
10 oz (275g) raw chicken, cut into pieces (skin removed if preferred)
8 oz (225g) streaky bacon pieces, chopped
1 large Spanish onion, chopped
2 cloves of garlic, crushed
8 oz (225g) tomatoes, skinned and seeded
1½ pt (900ml) water
2 chicken Oxo cubes
1 thimbleful of saffron powder or ½ level tsp turmeric
2 level tsp salt
Plenty of black pepper
1 lb (450g) long-grain rice
4 oz (100g) peeled prawns
4 oz (100g) frozen peas
12 whole prawns, in shell
8 oz (225g) green pepper, seeded and sliced
12 stuffed green olives
Lemon wedges
Cooked mussels (optional)

Cooking time: About 45 minutes.

Heat the oil in the paella pan. Add the chicken pieces and fry over medium heat for about 15 minutes, turning until brown on all sides. Add the bacon and onion and fry for a further 5 minutes.

Heat the oven to 350°F (180°C) mark 4.

Stir in the garlic, tomatoes, crumbled Oxo cubes, water and saffron and bring to the boil. Season with salt and freshly ground pepper and stir in the rice, peeled prawns and peas. Arrange the whole prawns and green pepper slices on top. Cover with a large piece of foil. Transfer to the oven and cook for about 45 minutes or until the rice is tender and all the stock is absorbed. Taste and check seasoning. Garnish with olives, lemon wedges and mussels (if used). Serve immediately.

Serves 8.

Top: Chicken Chi Chi *(recipe on page 170)*.
Bottom: Spanish Paella.

CHICKEN CHI CHI

This is the kind of chicken dish that you might make if you have bought some chicken joints and you have a small green pepper in the refrigerator. All the other ingredients are likely to be on the larder shelf.

Sauce

3 oz (75g) butter
1 large onion, sliced
1 small green pepper, chopped
2 level tbsp soft, dark brown sugar
5 level tbsp tomato ketchup
¼ pt (150ml) water
1 chicken Oxo cube, crumbled
2 tbsp vinegar
Juice of half a lemon
2 tbsp Worcestershire sauce
Salt and pepper

4 chicken portions

Cooking time: About 45 minutes.

To prepare the sauce: Melt 1 oz (25g) of butter in a saucepan, add the onion and green pepper and fry gently for 5 minutes. Add the remaining sauce ingredients and bring to the boil, stirring constantly. Reduce the heat and simmer uncovered for 15 minutes.

Meanwhile heat the oven to 350°F (180°C) mark 4.

Melt the remaining butter in a frying pan and quickly fry the chicken joints to brown on both sides. Lift them out and place in a single layer in a shallow heatproof dish. Pour over the sauce and cook in the oven for about 45 minutes or until the chicken is tender. Taste and check seasoning. Serve straight from the dish in which it was cooked.

Accompaniments: Serve with plain boiled rice and a tossed green salad.

Serves 4.

BALMORAL CHICKEN

To cut the chicken into portions you need a really sharp, large knife, but if time is short you can buy 8 chicken breasts.

3½-4 lb (1.5-1.8kg) roasting chicken
2 oz (50g) butter
2 tbsp oil
8 small onions, peeled and left whole
5 tbsp dry vermouth
Salt and pepper
1 bayleaf
8 oz (227g) can of peeled tomatoes
4 oz (100g) button mushrooms
A little chopped parsley (to garnish)

Cooking time: About 40 minutes.

Cut the legs and wings from the chicken and split each leg into two pieces at the joint. Remove the backbone from the carcass and split the breast in half lengthwise to make 8 joints in total.

Place the butter and oil in a large frying pan and fry the chicken over moderate heat to brown on both sides for 5-8 minutes. Add the onions when the first side of the chicken is brown and the chicken is turned over.

Pour the vermouth into the pan, add the salt, pepper, bayleaf and tomatoes and bring to the boil. Reduce the heat, cover the pan with a lid or foil and simmer very gently for 25 minutes.

Add the mushrooms to the pan and continue cooking for a further 15 minutes or until the chicken is tender. Arrange the chicken in a warm serving dish. Taste sauce and check seasoning. Remove the bayleaf. Pour the sauce over the chicken, sprinkle with chopped parsley and serve hot.

Accompaniments: Serve with new potatoes and peas.

Serves 8.

SPICED CHICKEN RISOTTO

Adding a little curry powder to a rice dish adds to the spiciness and yet doesn't make it taste of curry.

3 tbsp oil
4 chicken joints
2 onions, chopped
1 green pepper, seeded and cut in strips
8 oz (225g) long-grain rice
2 chicken Oxo cubes
About 1¼ pt (750ml) hot water
8 oz (227g) can of peeled tomatoes
1 clove of garlic, crushed
1 level tsp curry powder
4 oz (100g) mushrooms, sliced
Salt and pepper

Cooking time: About 45 minutes.

Heat the oil in a frying pan and fry the chicken joints quickly until golden brown on both sides. Reduce the heat, cover with a lid or foil and cook gently for about 20 minutes or until the chicken is tender. Lift it out and keep warm on one side.

Add the onions and green pepper to the pan and fry for 2-3 minutes or until soft. Add the rice and fry for a further 2-3 minutes. Crumble the Oxo cubes in the hot water, stir and add to the pan with the tomatoes, garlic and curry powder. Bring to the boil, stir lightly, then cover with a lid and simmer for about 25 minutes or until the rice is tender and all the stock is absorbed.

Stir in the mushrooms and cook for a further 5 minutes. Taste and check seasoning. Pile the rice onto a warm serving dish and arrange the chicken joints on top. Serve very hot.

Serves 4.

AMERICAN-STYLE BARBECUE CHICKEN

This is a very popular dish in our family: they all like the flavour and I like it because it is simple to prepare from ingredients that are to hand in the store cupboard. I find it's a very good natured dish which can quite easily be cooked under a cake or pastry on baking day, even at a slightly lower temperature. If you do this, increase the cooking time by about 15 minutes.

Salt and pepper
4 chicken joints
1 tbsp oil

Sauce
2 tbsp wine vinegar
2 tbsp soy sauce
1 level tbsp cornflour
1 tbsp Worcestershire sauce
2 level tsp castor sugar
4 tbsp tomato ketchup
4 tbsp water
1 clove of garlic, crushed

Cooking time: About 1 hour.

Heat the oven to 350°F (180°C) mark 4.

Season the chicken joints with salt and pepper. Heat the oil in a frying pan and quickly fry the chicken joints to brown. Lift them out and place in a shallow heatproof dish. Drain any oil from the pan. Blend together all the sauce ingredients and add to the pan. Bring to the boil, stirring until thickened. Spoon the sauce over the chicken. Cover with foil and cook in the oven for 45 minutes.

Remove the foil and cook for a further 15 minutes or until the chicken is tender. Serve straight from the dish in which it was cooked.

Accompaniments: Serve with plain boiled rice or buttered noodles and a tossed green salad.

Serves 4.

SCRUMPY CHICKEN

This is one of those quick recipes that are ideal to pop into the oven when time is running short. Cider goes well with chicken and helps to give it an excellent flavour.

1 oz (25g) plain flour
Salt and pepper
4 chicken joints
1 oz (25g) butter
1 tbsp oil
1 large onion, sliced
2 large tomatoes, skinned and chopped
4 oz (100g) mushrooms, sliced
10½ oz (298g) can of condensed chicken soup
¼ pt (150ml) dry cider

Cooking time: About 45 minutes.

Heat the oven to 350°F (180°C) mark 4.

Put the flour and seasoning in a bag, add the chicken joints and gently shake to coat them well with the seasoned flour.

Heat the butter and oil in a frying pan and fry the joints for about 5 minutes or until golden brown on both sides. Lift them out with a slotted spoon and place in a heatproof dish. Add the onion to the fat remaining in the pan and fry quickly to brown. Lift it out and place in the dish with the chicken. Place the tomatoes and mushrooms in the pan, then add the soup and cider. Bring to the boil, stirring constantly. Pour over the chicken, cover with a lid or foil and cook in the oven for about 45 minutes or until the chicken is quite tender. Taste and check seasoning. Serve straight from the dish in which it was cooked.

Accompaniments: Serve with new potatoes and green peas.

Serves 4.

Top: Scrumpy Chicken.
Bottom: Cidered Chicken with Mushrooms.

CIDERED CHICKEN WITH MUSHROOMS

This dish reheats very well once cooked, and may be cooled, covered and kept in the refrigerator for up to 24 hours.

3½ lb (1.5kg) chicken
½ pt (300ml) cider
1 onion, chopped
Salt and black pepper
Milk
2 oz (50g) butter
2 oz (50g) plain flour
½ lb (225g) button mushrooms, sliced
Fresh parsley (to garnish)

Cooking time: About 1¾ hours.

Heat the oven to 350°F (180°C) mark 4.

Place the chicken and giblets in a small roasting tin or casserole, add the cider and onion and season well with salt and freshly ground pepper. Cover with a lid or foil and cook in the oven for 20 minutes per lb (450g) plus an extra 20 minutes (i.e. about 1½ hours). To test if the chicken is cooked, pierce the thickest part of the leg with a skewer: if clear juices run out, the bird is cooked. Lift it out onto a plate to cool. Strain off the remaining liquid in the tin, skim off the fat and make up to 1¼ pt (750ml) with milk.

Chop the chicken liver. Remove the meat from the bird and cut into good sized pieces, then add the liver. Use the carcass and the giblets to make stock for soup on another occasion.

Melt the butter in a saucepan, add the flour and cook for 2 minutes without colouring. Stir in the stock and milk, slowly at first, and bring to the boil. Add the mushrooms and season with plenty of salt and pepper. Stir in the chicken pieces and turn into a warm serving dish when piping hot. Garnish with parsley.

Accompaniments: For a special occasion, serve with crispy fried bread triangles arranged around the dish.

Serves 6.

FRENCH ROAST CHICKEN

Cooking chicken in this way keeps it very moist and gives it a good flavour. If you don't have fresh herbs in the garden, use a teaspoonful of dried mixed herbs instead.

3½ lb (1.5kg) roasting chicken (with giblets)
1½ oz (40g) butter
1 small bunch of fresh mixed herbs
½ pt (300ml) hot water
1 chicken Oxo cube
1 oz (25g) cornflour
1 tbsp cold water

Cooking time: About 1¼ hours.

Heat the oven to 350°F (180°C) mark 4.

Wipe the chicken inside and out and place two-thirds of the butter and the bunch of herbs inside it. Place the chicken in a roasting tin and cover the breast with the remaining butter. Cover with a piece of greaseproof paper. Add the giblets to the roasting tin. Crumble the Oxo cube in the hot water, stir and pour into the tin. Cook in the oven for 30 minutes, then remove the greaseproof paper and turn the chicken to allow it to brown all over. First turn it on its side and cook for a further 45 minutes, turning every 15 minutes until tender. Remove from the oven and place on a warm serving dish. Remove the herbs.

Blend the cornflour with the cold water and stir into the stock in the roasting tin. Bring to the boil, stirring constantly, then simmer for 2 minutes. Taste and check seasoning. Strain the sauce into a sauce boat.

Accompaniments: This makes a delicious meal at any time of the year; in summer, serve with buttered new potatoes and green beans, and in winter with roast potatoes and carrots or Brussels sprouts.

Serves 5-6.

Top: French Roast Chicken.
Bottom: Coq au Vin.

COQ AU VIN

This dish is even better if it is made the day before it is required and then reheated in a moderate oven for about 45 minutes, as this gives the chicken a delicious flavour.

6 chicken portions
1½ oz (40g) seasoned flour
1 oz (25g) butter
1 tbsp oil
4 oz (100g) piece of streaky bacon, cut into strips
8 oz (225g) button onions
1 chicken Oxo cube
½ pt (300ml) hot water
¼ pt (150ml) inexpensive red wine
1 rounded tbsp tomato purée
Salt and pepper
6 oz (175g) button mushrooms

Cooking time: About 1 hour.

Heat the oven to 350°F (180°C) mark 4.

Remove the skin from each chicken joint if preferred and coat the joints in flour. Heat the butter and oil in a large frying pan, add the chicken joints and fry until brown on all sides. Lift them out with a slotted spoon and place in a heat-proof casserole. Add the bacon strips and button onions to the pan and fry gently for 5 minutes. Lift them out with a slotted spoon and add to the chicken joints.

Stir the remaining flour into the pan and cook for 1 minute. Crumble the Oxo cube in the hot water and stir. Add to the pan with the wine and tomato purée and bring to the boil, stirring until the sauce has thickened. Season well with salt and pepper and pour over the chicken. Cover with a lid or foil and cook in the oven for 45 minutes. Stir in the mushrooms, return to the oven and cook for a further 15 minutes or until the chicken is tender. Taste and check seasoning.

Accompaniments: Serve with Duchesse potatoes and garden peas.

Serves 6.

CHICKEN IN A POT

Since all the vegetables in this recipe are cooked in one large casserole with the chicken, the washing up is made so much simpler!

1 oz (25g) butter
8 oz (225g) carrots, sliced
8 oz (225g) button onions, peeled and left whole
4 oz (100g) streaky bacon, cut into strips
3½ lb (1.5kg) oven-ready chicken
¼ pt (150ml) water
1 chicken Oxo cube
Salt and pepper
1¼ lb (550g) small or medium potatoes, quartered lengthwise

Cooking time: About 1¾ hours.

Heat the oven to 350°F (180°C) mark 4.

Melt the butter in a frying pan. Add the carrots, onions and bacon and fry gently for about 8 minutes or until the three ingredients are pale golden brown and the fat has run out of the bacon. Lift them out with a slotted spoon and place in a large 5 pt (2.8l) heatproof casserole.

Add the chicken to the fat remaining in the pan and fry quickly to brown on all sides. Lift it out and place on top of the vegetables in the casserole. Add the water and crumbled Oxo cube to the pan and bring to the boil, stirring constantly. Pour over the chicken and season well with salt and pepper. Cover with a tight-fitting lid or foil and cook in the oven for 45 minutes.

Add the potatoes to the casserole, ensuring that they are well covered by the stock. Return to the oven and cook for a further hour or until the chicken is tender. Lift out the chicken and place on a warm serving dish. Spoon some of the vegetables around and serve the remainder separately.

Accompaniments: If you like a lot of vegetables, you might serve this with peas which are quick and simple to cook.

Serves 4-6.

TALLIS CHICKEN

In season, use fresh, ripe tomatoes for this recipe instead of canned ones and, if necessary, add a little extra stock when cooking the rice.

4 oz (100g) long-grain rice
2 tbsp oil
4 chicken portions
Salt and pepper
1 large onion, sliced
8 oz (227g) can of peeled tomatoes
1 chicken Oxo cube
¾ pt (450ml) water
1 tsp fresh, chopped thyme

Cooking time: About 50-60 minutes.

Heat the oven to 350°F (180°C) mark 4.

Place the rice in the bottom of a shallow 3 pt (1.7l) heatproof dish. Heat the oil in a frying pan and fry the chicken portions until lightly browned on both sides. Lift them out and arrange on top of the rice. Season very well with salt and pepper.

Drain any oil from the pan, then add the onion, tomatoes, crumbled Oxo cube, water and thyme. Bring to the boil, stirring constantly until well blended. Pour over the chicken, cover with a lid or foil and cook in the oven for 50-60 minutes or until the rice and chicken are tender.

Accompaniments: Since the rice is cooked with this dish, a green salad is all you need to accompany it.

Serves 4.

Top: Chicken in a Pot.
Bottom: Tallis Chicken.

LEMON CHICKEN

This is nice if served hot, but is equally popular if served cold with a variety of salads on a picnic.

Marinade

Grated rind and juice of 1 lemon
2 tbsp oil
1 tbsp soy sauce
1 clove of garlic, crushed
1 level tsp salt
Freshly ground black pepper

8 chicken drumsticks
3 level tbsp plain flour
2 level tsp paprika pepper
2 oz (50g) butter, melted
Lemon twists (to garnish)

Cooking time: About 35 minutes.

Mix together all the marinade ingredients. Place the drumsticks in a dish and pour over the marinade. Cover and allow to stand in a cool place for at least 2 hours.

Heat the oven to 400°F (200°C) mark 6.

Blend together the flour and paprika pepper in a bag. Lift the drumsticks from the marinade and coat with the flour and paprika pepper mixture. Arrange in a single layer in a heatproof dish, pour over the melted butter and bake in the oven for 20 minutes.

Pour over the marinade and bake for a further 15 minutes. Garnish with twisted slices of lemon, and serve straight from the dish in which they were cooked.

Accompaniments: If hot, serve with sauté potatoes, baked tomatoes and peas; if cold, with a variety of salads.

Serves 4.

See photograph on back of book for Lemon Chicken (top) and Chinese Chicken (bottom).

CHINESE CHICKEN

This recipe can be made with fillet of pork, prawns or shrimps instead of chicken. It also makes an excellent filling for savoury pancakes (see page 79).

12 oz (350g) breast of chicken
12 oz (350g) white cabbage
6 spring onions
2 level tsp cornflour
2 tbsp sherry
2 tbsp corn oil
Salt
Black pepper
1 green pepper, seeded and thinly sliced
8 oz (225g) bean sprouts
1 clove of garlic, crushed
1 chicken Oxo cube
¼ pt (150ml) hot water
2 tbsp soy sauce

Cooking time: About 8-10 minutes.

Slice the chicken into fine pencil-thin strips about 2 in. (5cm) long. Shred the cabbage finely. Cut the spring onions into 2 in. (5cm) lengths. Blend the cornflour with the sherry.

Heat the oil in a wok or large heavy saucepan until very hot. Season the chicken with salt and freshly ground pepper, add to the pan and cook over fierce heat for 1 minute, constantly tossing and moving the chicken about the pan. Lift it out with a slotted spoon and arrange on a plate.

Reheat the wok or pan and add the cabbage, green pepper, bean sprouts, spring onions and garlic. Cook for 3-4 minutes, tossing constantly. Return the chicken to the pan. Crumble the Oxo cube in the hot water, stir and add to the pan with the soy sauce and blended cornflour. Cook for at least 1 minute or until the liquid is creamy and the vegetables are still crisp. Taste and check seasoning.

Accompaniments: Serve this dish on its own or with plain boiled rice.

Serves 4.

OFFAL

RECIPES

The classic offal dish of haggis (cook as instructed on the pack). Serve with the traditional accompaniments of mashed potatoes and swede.

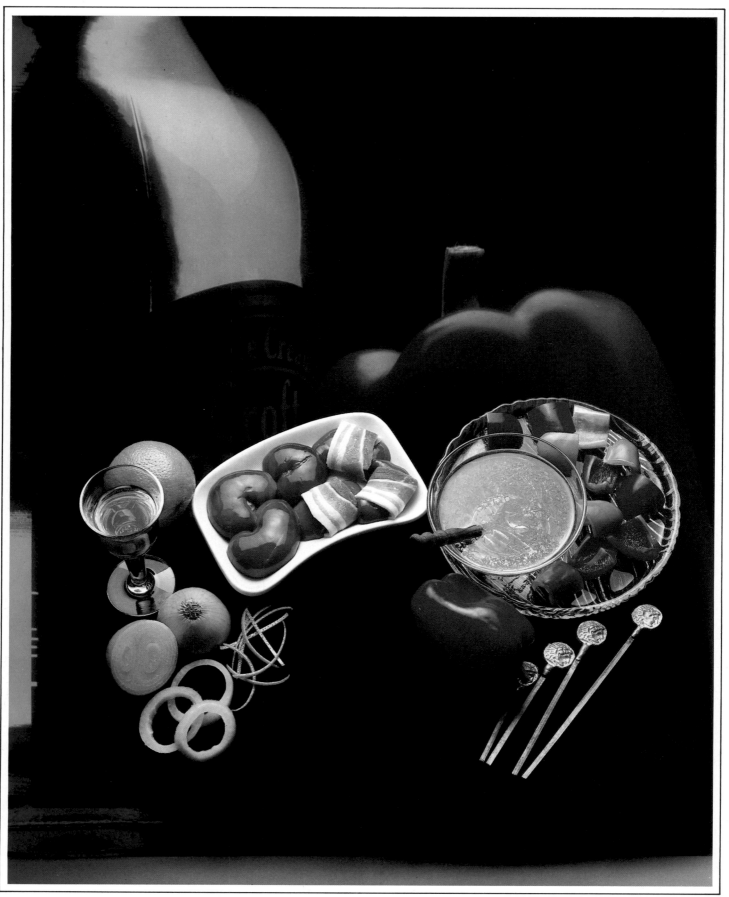

MARINATED KIDNEY KEBABS

A marinade gives a lovely flavour and helps to soften the fibres of tougher meats. Lambs' kidneys cook quickly, and are especially good grilled with bacon.

Marinade
2 tbsp oil
4 tbsp dry vermouth
½ level tsp dried thyme or 1 level tsp fresh, chopped thyme leaves
1 level tsp salt
Freshly ground black pepper

8 lambs' kidneys
8 streaky bacon rashers
1 large red pepper
1 large green pepper

Cooking time: About 15 minutes.

Mix together all the marinade ingredients. Cut each kidney in half, then use scissors to remove the core. Place the kidneys in a container and pour over the marinade. Cover with a tight-fitting lid, and turn the container upside down to coat the kidneys with the marinade. Leave to stand for 6-12 hours, turning occasionally.

Strain the kidneys, reserving the marinade. Remove the bacon rind. Stretch the rashers with a round-bladed knife until they are double their length, then cut in half. Wrap each half piece of bacon round each half of kidney. Cut the peppers in half and remove the core and seeds. Cut the flesh into 20 pieces of red pepper and 20 pieces of green.

With long thin skewers, pierce first a piece of red pepper, then a piece of green pepper, then a wrapped kidney. Repeat, using 5 pieces of each pepper (i.e. 10 pieces of pepper in total) and 4 wrapped kidneys on each skewer.

Left: Ingredients for Sherried Kidneys.
Right: Ingredients for Marinated Kidney Kebabs.

Place the kebabs in a grill pan and brush with a little of the marinade. Cook under a moderately hot grill for 7-8 minutes. Turn the kebabs over, brush again with marinade and grill for a further 8 minutes. Remove from the pan and keep hot. Pour the remaining marinade into the pan and heat, blending with the juices from the kebabs.

Accompaniments: Serve with special kebab rice (see page 60), and the marinade sauce poured over the top.

Serves 4.

SHERRIED KIDNEYS

These make an ideal light lunch or supper dish.

8 lambs' kidneys
2 oz (50g) butter
1 onion, thinly sliced
1 oz (25g) plain flour
½ pt (300ml) water
1 chicken Oxo cube
Salt and black pepper
4 tbsp sherry

Cooking time: About 12-15 minutes.

Peel off the thin skin from each kidney. Hold the kidney under your left hand and horizontally cut through so that the kidney is cut in half. Use scissors to remove the core.

Melt 1 oz (25g) of butter in a frying pan, add the kidneys and fry gently for 2-3 minutes. Lift them out with a slotted spoon and put on a plate. Add the remaining butter and the onion to the pan and fry for 5 minutes or until soft and golden brown. Stir in the flour and cook for 1 minute, blend in the water and crumbled Oxo cube and bring to the boil, stirring constantly until the sauce has thickened. Add the salt, freshly ground pepper and sherry to the sauce and return the kidneys to the pan with any juices on the plate. Simmer gently for about 5 minutes or until just tender. Taste and check seasoning. Turn into a warm serving dish.

Accompaniments: Serve with plain boiled rice and grilled bacon rolls.

Serves 4.

CANTERBURY CASSEROLE

Lambs' hearts are inexpensive and taste very good if carefully cooked. You need a pair of good kitchen scissors or a small sharp kitchen knife to cut out the tubes.

3-4 lambs' hearts
1 oz (25g) seasoned flour
A good knob of dripping
2 carrots, sliced
2 onions, sliced
3 outside sticks of celery, sliced
1 pt (600ml) water
1 red Oxo cube

Parsley dumplings
4 oz (100g) self-raising flour
A generous pinch of salt
2 oz (50g) shredded suet
1 level tbsp chopped parsley
About 6 tbsp water

Cooking time: About 2 hours.

Cut out the tubes from the hearts with scissors or a sharp knife. Cut into slices and then into ½ in. (1.25cm) pieces. Coat in seasoned flour. Melt the dripping in a saucepan and fry the hearts until brown on all sides. Add the remaining flour and vegetables and fry for 3-4 minutes. Stir in the water and crumbled Oxo cube and bring to the boil, stirring constantly. Cover with a lid, reduce the heat to simmer for 1½ hours or until the hearts are nearly tender. Taste and check seasoning.

Meanwhile prepare the dumplings: Mix the flour, salt, suet and parsley in a bowl, then add sufficient water to make a soft dough. Form into 8 balls. Place on top of the casserole, recover with the lid and continue cooking very gently for about 30 minutes or until well risen. Turn into a warm serving dish and serve immediately.

Accompaniments: Serve with boiled potatoes or two vegetables such as buttered cabbage and parsnips.

Serves 4.

CRISP SWEETBREADS

Prepare the sweetbreads in advance and leave in the refrigerator until you require them – they can then be served in about 5 minutes.

1 lb (450g) lamb's sweetbreads
Water
1 chicken Oxo cube
1 egg, beaten
Fresh white breadcrumbs
2 oz (50g) butter
4 back bacon rashers or 8 streaky bacon rashers (with rind removed)
1 sprig of parsley (to garnish)

Cooking time: About 5 minutes.

Soak the sweetbreads in very cold water for about 2 hours to remove all the blood, then drain well. Place in a saucepan, cover with fresh water and add 1 tsp of salt. Bring to the boil very slowly (allow at least 5 minutes, or longer if possible), then drain off the water again. Carefully remove any membrane without tearing the sweetbreads.

Rinse out the pan, then add the sweetbreads, crumbled Oxo cube and sufficient water to cover the sweetbreads. Simmer for 15-20 minutes or until the sweetbreads are tender. Drain well and allow to become quite cold.

Cut any very large sweetbreads in half at an angle and coat in the beaten egg and fresh white breadcrumbs. Melt the butter in a frying pan and fry the sweetbreads very gently until evenly browned, turning once. Meanwhile cook the bacon under a moderate grill. Lift out the sweetbreads, arrange on a warm serving dish with the rashers of grilled bacon and garnish with the sprig of parsley. Serve immediately.

Accompaniments: Serve with grilled tomatoes and French beans.

Serves 4.

Top: Canterbury Casserole.
Bottom: Crisp Sweetbreads.

LIVER IN PIQUANT SAUCE

Pig's liver is suggested for this recipe as it is usually the least expensive of the livers available. It has a slightly stronger flavour which becomes milder if you pre-soak it in milk, but use lamb's liver if you prefer. A common mistake with liver is to overcook it, so follow the cooking instructions carefully.

1 lb (450g) pig's liver
8 oz (225g) onions
2 oz (50g) dripping
2 oz (50g) plain flour
1 pt (600ml) water
1 red Oxo cube
3 tbsp tomato ketchup
¼ level tsp dried marjoram
1 level tsp Worcestershire sauce
Salt and pepper
Fresh, chopped parsley (to garnish)

Cooking time: About 30 minutes.

Cut the liver into long strips about ½ in. (1.25cm) wide, soak in a little milk for 30 minutes, then drain.

Meanwhile peel and slice the onions. Melt the dripping in a saucepan, add the onions and fry for 5-10 minutes until golden brown. Stir in the flour and cook for 2 minutes. Add the water and crumbled Oxo cube and bring to the boil, stirring until thickened. Add the ketchup, marjoram, Worcestershire sauce, salt and pepper. Stir well, cover with a lid and simmer gently for about 20 minutes.

Add the strips of liver to the hot sauce and cook gently for about 10 minutes or until just cooked. Sprinkle with parsley. Serve immediately.

Accompaniments: Serve with creamy mashed potatoes to soak up the sauce, and sliced carrots.

Serves 4.

BAKED LIVER DUMPLINGS

With the high prices of meat these days, this is an interesting way to make a little go a long way. Bacon, or cheese and tomato, could be used as an alternative to liver.

4 oz (100g) self-raising flour
2 oz (50g) shredded suet
1 level tsp salt
1 level tsp dried sage
Black pepper
6 oz (175g) lamb's liver
1 egg
1 tbsp water
1 oz (25g) beef dripping

Cooking time: About 25 minutes.

Heat the oven to 375°F (190°C) mark 5.

Put the flour, suet, sage and freshly ground pepper in a bowl. Cut the liver into thin strips, then dice into small cubes about ¼ in. (0.6cm) square. Add it to the other ingredients in the bowl. Beat together the egg and water and add to the bowl. Stir together to a stiff mixture.

Place a little dripping in the bottom of 8 bun tins and heat in the oven until melted. Divide the dumpling mixture equally between the bun tins (there is no need to smooth the mixture since the dumplings should have a slightly roughened appearance, like rock cakes). Bake in the oven for about 25 minutes or until crisp and lightly browned. Serve hot.

Accompaniments: Serve with onion gravy (see page 59), a green vegetable and buttered carrots.

Serves 4.

Top: Liver in Piquant Sauce.
Bottom: Baked Liver Dumplings.

BRAISED STUFFED HEARTS

Any well-flavoured stuffing goes with hearts, but I find this one, with plenty of grated lemon rind, is very good. There is no need to use the vegetables as given in the recipe: ring the changes by using whatever you have in the vegetable basket.

4 lambs' hearts

Stuffing
2 oz (50g) fresh white breadcrumbs
Grated rind of half a small lemon
1 level tbsp chopped parsley
½ level tbsp chopped thyme
2 tbsp milk
Salt and pepper

3 carrots, sliced
2 onions, chopped
2 sticks of celery, sliced
1 parsnip, diced
1 oz (25g) dripping
¾ pt (450ml) water
1 red Oxo cube
1 level tbsp cornflour

Cooking time: About 1¾ hours.

Wash the hearts thoroughly and leave to soak in salted water for 30 minutes. Use scissors or a sharp knife to remove the tubes. Mix together all the stuffing ingredients in a bowl and use to fill the cavities in the hearts.

Heat the oven to 350°F (180°C) mark 4.

Top: Braised Stuffed Hearts.
Bottom: Fried Brains.

Place all the vegetables in the bottom of a 3 pt (1.7l) heatproof casserole. Melt the dripping in a frying pan and fry the hearts lightly on all sides to brown. Lift them out and place on top of the vegetables. Drain any dripping from the pan, add the water and crumbled Oxo cube and bring to the boil, stirring until well blended. Pour into the casserole. Cover with a lid or foil and cook in the oven for about 1¾ hours or until the hearts are tender.

Lift out the hearts and arrange on a warm serving dish with the vegetables around. Blend the cornflour with a little cold water and stir into the casserole until the sauce thickens. Return to the oven for 2-3 minutes to cook, then pour the sauce over the hearts.

Accompaniments: Serve this casserole with plain boiled potatoes or with jacket potatoes, cooked in the oven beside the casserole.

Serves 4.

FRIED BRAINS

Fried brains need to be eaten as soon as they are cooked otherwise they lose their crispness. They are good without tartar sauce, too: simply serve them on toast as you would fried herring roes.

1½ lb (675g) calf's or lamb's brains
1 small onion
¼ level tsp salt
Vinegar
Seasoned flour
2 eggs, beaten
Oil (for frying)
Tartar sauce (see page 58)
Lemon wedges

Cooking time: 5 minutes.

Soak the brains in cold water for 30 minutes, then rinse under cold running water and drain well. Remove any arteries and membranes with a pointed knife and make sure that the brains are free of any trace of blood.

Fried Brains continued from page 186.

Place the brains in a saucepan, cover with cold water and add 2 tbsp of vinegar to each 1½ pt (900ml) of water used. Add the onion and salt and cook slowly until boiling gently. Reduce the heat and simmer for 5 minutes or until tender. Drain the brains and plunge into cold water. Roll the brains in seasoned flour, dip in the beaten egg and shallow fry until pale golden brown. Lift them out with a slotted spoon and drain on kitchen paper. Arrange on a hot serving dish and serve with tartar sauce and lemon wedges.

Accompaniments: Fried brains are nice served with a tossed green salad and chunks of warm French bread.

Serves 6.

FAST-FRIED LIVER

Lamb's liver is so tender that it cooks very quickly. This dish can be prepared and cooked while the table is being laid!

2 tbsp oil
1 lb (450g) lamb's liver
10 oz (275g) frozen mixed vegetables
1 level tsp salt
Black pepper
1 tbsp soy sauce
2 level tsp brown sugar
1 tbsp chopped parsley

Cooking time: About 7-10 minutes.

Cut the liver into thin strips. Heat the oil in a large sauté pan or frying pan. Fry the liver on high heat for about 3 minutes, turning it to seal the strips on all sides. Add the vegetables (lift the pan off the heat while you do this, as the cold vegetables may make the fat spit a bit). Add the salt and freshly ground pepper and fry on high heat for about 4 minutes, stirring lightly all the time. Stir in the soy sauce, sugar and parsley.

Accompaniments: Serve on a bed of boiled rice or noodles.

Serves 4.

CREAMED SWEETBREADS

It is most important to soak sweetbreads in very cold water before parboiling them, as this helps to remove all the blood and keeps the sweetbreads white.

1½ lb (675g) calf's sweetbreads
1 sprig of lemon thyme
½ pt (300ml) water
1 chicken Oxo cube
¼ pt (150ml) dry white wine
Salt and black pepper
4 oz (100g) very small button mushrooms
2½ oz (62g) butter
2 oz (50g) plain flour
¼ pt (150ml) single cream
Chopped parsley (to garnish)

Cooking time: About 30 minutes.

Soak the sweetbreads in very cold water for about 2 hours to remove all the blood, then drain well. Place them in a saucepan, cover with fresh water and add 1 tsp of salt. Bring to the boil very slowly (allow at least 5 minutes, or longer if possible), then drain off the water again. Carefully remove any membrane without tearing the sweetbreads.

Rinse out the pan, then add the sweetbreads with the lemon thyme, ½ pt (300ml) water and the crumbled Oxo cube, wine, salt and freshly ground pepper. Bring to the boil, cover with a lid and simmer for 10 minutes. Add the button mushrooms and cook for a further 5 minutes. Strain the cooking liquor into a measuring jug, remove the thyme and keep the sweetbreads and mushrooms on one side.

Melt the butter in a saucepan, add the flour and cook for 1 minute. Blend in the cooking liquor and bring to the boil, stirring until thickened. Simmer for 2 minutes. Return the sweetbreads and mushrooms to the pan and reheat until hot through. Taste and check seasoning. Stir in the cream and sprinkle with chopped parsley. Serve immediately.

Accompaniments: This dish is ideal served with buttered spinach or broccoli and plain boiled rice.

Serves 6.

TRIPE AND ONIONS

Tripe has already been cooked and prepared by the butcher when you buy it, so there is no need to cook it for very long.

1½ lb (675g) tripe

---

1 pt (600ml) milk

---

1 level tsp salt

---

1 bayleaf

---

1 lb (450g) onions, quartered

Sauce

---

1 oz (25g) butter

---

1 oz (25g) plain flour

---

2 tsp chopped parsley

Pepper

Cooking time: About 2 hours.

Cut the tripe into 1½ in. (3.5cm) squares. Place it in a large saucepan, cover with cold water and bring to the boil. Simmer for 5 minutes, then drain. Add to the saucepan the milk, salt and bayleaf and simmer for 1¼ hours. Add the onions and continue cooking for a further 45 minutes.

To make the sauce: Melt the butter in a saucepan, stir in the flour and cook for 1 minute. Drain the milk from the tripe and gradually stir it into the pan. Bring to the boil, stirring until thickened. Stir in the parsley and season well with pepper. Remove the bayleaf from the tripe. Stir the tripe and onions into the sauce and heat through until piping hot. Taste and check seasoning. Turn into a warm serving dish and serve immediately.

Accompaniments: Serve with mashed potatoes and mixed root vegetables, including carrots, to add a little colour.

Serves 4-6.

OXTAIL

Oxtail has a very rich flavour and is inclined to be fatty. If possible, it is best to cook it the day before you need it, then let it get quite cold. The fat will then come to the surface so you can easily remove it. Take care to simmer the oxtail gently once it has come to the boil, for fast boiling spoils the flavour and shrinks the meat.

---

1 oxtail, jointed (about 2½ lb [1.1kg] in weight)

1½ oz (40g) dripping

---

1 oz (25g) plain flour

---

1 pt (600ml) water

---

1 red Oxo cube

---

2 onions, chopped

---

2 carrots, chopped

---

2 sticks of celery, chopped

About 1½ level tsp salt

Plenty of black pepper

¼ level tsp cayenne pepper

---

1 bayleaf

Cooking time: About 3½-4 hours.

Trim any excess fat from the oxtail. Heat the dripping in a large saucepan and quickly fry the oxtail on all sides to brown. Lift it out with a slotted spoon and keep on one side.

Stir the flour into the fat remaining in the pan and cook for 1 minute. Blend in the water and the crumbled Oxo cube and bring to the boil, stirring until the sauce has thickened.

Return the oxtail to the pan with the vegetables, salt, freshly ground pepper, cayenne pepper and bayleaf. Cover with a lid or foil and simmer very gently for 3½-4 hours or until the meat can be easily removed from the bones. Skim off any surplus fat. Taste and check seasoning. Remove the bayleaf. Turn into a warm serving dish and serve immediately.

Accompaniments: Serve with plain boiled potatoes and cabbage.

Serves 4-6.

HEARTS IN SWEET AND SOUR SAUCE

Cooking the hearts slowly in the spicy sauce gives them an excellent flavour and makes them so tender. I like to soak the hearts in salted water and then blanch them as I find it helps to remove all the blood.

4 lambs' hearts

Sauce

2 tbsp oil

3 carrots, cut in long strips

1 leek, finely sliced

2 sticks of celery, sliced

1 level tbsp cornflour

2 level tsp light brown sugar

½ pt (300ml) water

2 tbsp tomato ketchup

1 tbsp vinegar

2 tbsp soy sauce

Salt and pepper

Cooking time: About 1½ hours.

Soak the hearts in lightly salted water for 30 minutes. Place them in a saucepan with fresh water and bring to the boil. Drain them, then cut in half lengthwise. Use scissors or a sharp knife to remove the tubes. Cut the flesh into ¼ in. (0.6cm) slices.

Heat the oil in a saucepan and quickly fry the heart strips for 3 minutes. Lift them out with a slotted spoon and place on a plate. Add the carrots, leek and celery to the pan and fry for 2 minutes.

Put the cornflour and sugar in a bowl and gradually stir in the water. Add the ketchup, vinegar and soy sauce. Pour into the pan and bring to the boil, stirring until thickened. Add the salt and pepper and return the hearts to the pan. Cover with a lid and simmer for about 1½ hours or until the hearts are tender. Taste and check seasoning. Turn into a warm serving dish and serve immediately.

Accompaniments: Serve with boiled noodles or rice.

Serves 4.

HOME-COOKED OX TONGUE

Home-cooked ox tongue is more economical than the shop variety. If you are cooking for just one or two people, use pig's or sheep's tongue instead. Cook it until just tender, usually about 1 hour, then prepare as detailed below and pack into margarine tubs.

1 ox tongue (about 3½ lb [1.5kg] in weight), salt or pickled

1 onion, peeled and stuck with 1 clove

2 bayleaves

1 large sprig of parsley

Cooking time: About 3¼–3¾ hours.

Soak the tongue in water for 24 hours, changing the water several times. Drain off the water and place in a saucepan with fresh cold water to cover. Add the onion, bayleaves and parsley and bring to the boil. Cover with a lid or foil and simmer gently for 3¼-3¾ hours, topping up with boiling water when necessary to keep the tongue covered.

To test if the tongue is cooked, pierce the tip with a fine skewer: it will feel tender if it is cooked. Drain and plunge immediately into a bowl of cold water. Remove the skin, bones and gristle. Place the tongue on a board and cut in half lengthwise. Place one half, cut side downwards, in a round 6 in. (15cm) cake tin, curling it slightly to fit, then arrange the second half, cut side uppermost, on top. Cover with a saucer and place a heavy weight on top (a small saucepan filled with cold water makes an effective weight).

Usually sufficient jelly will set around the tongue so no extra will be required. However, ½ pt (300ml) of cooking liquor from the pan may be boiled rapidly for 3-4 minutes to reduce it to about ¼ pt (150ml) and then spooned over the tongue.

Allow to become quite cold then chill in the refrigerator overnight. Turn out onto a plate and serve garnished with salads.

Serves 10-12.

Left: Hearts in Sweet and Sour Sauce.
Right: Home-cooked Ox Tongue.

BOAR'S HEAD

Using a pig's head is a bit of a cheat, but makes a very effective centre piece for a buffet table. *It is not to be eaten.* It is easy enough to buy a pig's head at a reasonable price from a good butcher. Ask him to prepare it by removing the hair from the skin and trimming the back of the head short at the neck. Make sure you have a large enough pan in which to cook the head (see Old-fashioned Cooked Ham page 150)).

1 pig's head (not a boar's head, as these are difficult to obtain)
3 oz (75g) gelatine
¾ pt (450ml) water
2 red Oxo cubes
About 6 oz (175g) lard
1 rosy red apple
About 6 oz (175g) lard
2 glass eyes (teddy bear's eyes bought from a haberdasher's or toy shop)
Eyelashes (optional) Use false eyelashes, or green, feathery fern trimmed off on one side, or yew leaves

Cooking time: About 3 hours.

Open the pig's mouth and keep it open by inserting a block of wood. Lift the pig's head into the large saucepan and support the ears with foil, bending them inwards if necessary to get the pan lid on. Cover with cold water and a lid, bring to the boil and simmer very gently for 3 hours. Place the pan in a cool place and allow to cool overnight. (I made this in the winter and left it outside the back door, tying on the lid so that the cat did not get it.)

The following day, drain off the water and remove the block of wood from the pig's mouth. Chill for several hours in the refrigerator or for 1 hour in the freezer, so it becomes really cold (which is necessary to enable the glaze to set quickly).

To make the glaze: Soak the gelatine in ¼ pt (150ml) of the water for about 5 minutes or until it becomes sponge-like. Add the remaining ½ pt (300ml) of water and cook gently over low heat until clear. Crumble the Oxo cubes, add to the pan and stir well. Remove the pan from the heat and leave to cool but do not allow to set.

Remove the pig's head from the fridge or freezer and wipe with kitchen paper to remove any loose pieces of skin. Brush with the glaze. (This should set as it comes into contact with the skin if the pig is really cold. If not, chill the jelly a little more but do not allow it to set; if this happens, reheat the jelly and start again.)

Place the apple in the pig's mouth. Press in the eyes on their wires. If used, attach the eyelashes with a little glue, if necessary. (I used yew leaves, trimmed off on one side to look like lashes, and they stuck on their own.)

Soften the lard slightly and cream with a wooden spatula. Put a medium rose nozzle in a piping bag and fill with the lard. Pipe a line around the edge of each ear, an S-shape on each cheek, a line around the nose and a few fancy shapes elsewhere. Cover a round tray or board with foil and lift the head onto it. Garnish the dish with parsley sprigs or evergreen leaves.

When the party is over, if the pig's head is still fresh, it can be stripped of the glaze, re-boiled for 1½ hours and made into brawn.

Boar's Head.

CHICKEN LIVERS MARSALA

Marsala and Madeira are fortified wines and are similar in flavour. Both are excellent in kidney and liver dishes. Sherry gives an almost identical taste, so use whatever you have in the house.

| 1 lb (450g) chicken livers |
| 1 oz (25g) plain flour |
| 1 level tsp salt |
| Black pepper |
| ¼ level tsp marjoram |
| 2 oz (50g) butter |
| 8 spring onions, chopped |
| 6 oz (175g) mushrooms, sliced |
| 1 chicken Oxo cube |
| ¼ pt (150ml) hot water |
| 3 fl oz (75ml) Marsala, Madeira or sherry |

Cooking time: About 15 minutes.

Toss the chicken livers with the flour, salt, freshly ground pepper and marjoram. Melt the butter in a large frying pan, add the onions and mushrooms and lightly fry for 2 minutes. Add the chicken livers and cook for about 10 minutes, stirring gently and turning until just cooked through, and no longer pink on the outside. Crumble the Oxo cube in the hot water and stir. Pour into the pan, then add the wine. Taste and check seasoning. Serve immediately.

Accompaniments: Arrange the chicken livers on a bed of hot, fluffy boiled rice. A good vegetable to serve with this dish would be either leaf spinach or whole green beans.

Serves 4.

ITALIAN LIVER

This is a simple way of serving liver that is quick to cook and attractive to serve.

| 4-6 oz (100-175g) button mushrooms, chopped |
| 2 level tbsp chopped parsley |
| 1 level tbsp chopped chives |
| 1 small clove of garlic, crushed |
| 1 lb (450g) lamb's liver, sliced |
| Seasoned flour |
| 2 tbsp oil |
| 2 oz (50g) butter |
| 2 tbsp lemon juice |
| Black pepper |

Cooking time: About 6 minutes.

Put the mushrooms, parsley, chives and garlic in a bowl and mix together. Coat the liver with the seasoned flour. Heat the oil and butter in a frying pan and quickly fry the liver for about 3 minutes, turning once. Lift it out and keep warm on a serving dish. Add the mushrooms and herbs to the fat remaining in the pan and cook for 3 minutes. Stir in the lemon juice and plenty of freshly ground pepper. Pour over the liver and serve immediately.

Accompaniments: Serve with spinach and sauté potatoes.

Serves 4.

GAME
RECIPES

Classic roast pheasant (see page 37 for roasting instructions).
Serve with the traditional accompaniments of fried
breadcrumbs (see page 37) and game chips.

PIGEON PIE

Late August and September are the best months in which to buy fresh pigeons as the birds are at their fattest then. If ever you are given pigeons straight from 'the shoot', prepare them by plucking the breast and using this meat only. Discard the rest – there is very little meat on the legs and wings. Prepared pigeons can sometimes be found in butchers' shops or in supermarket freezers. Use the whole birds in this case. After cooking them, pick the meat from the bones – either before making the pie, or actually at the table.

If you plan to make the pie using whole pigeons, you will need a pie dish about 3 pt (1.7l) in capacity. If you haven't got one this size, use the largest pie dish you have, cut the meat off the birds after cooking them and mix with the steak before baking in the oven.

4 wood pigeons, prepared as above
1 oz (25g) butter
2 tbsp oil
8 oz (225g) stewing steak, cut into cubes
16 button onions, peeled and left whole
4 oz (100g) mushrooms, sliced
½ pt (300ml) inexpensive red wine
1 bayleaf (optional)
2 tbsp redcurrant jelly
1 level tsp dried thyme
2 level tsp salt
Black pepper
1 red Oxo cube
½ pt (300ml) hot water
Pastry
8 oz (225g) self-raising flour
4 oz (100g) shredded suet
½ level tsp salt
About ¼ pt (150ml) water
1 egg, beaten (to glaze)

Cooking time: About 3 hours.

Wash the pigeons and dry them thoroughly on kitchen paper. Heat the butter and oil in a frying pan and fry the pigeons over fairly high heat on all sides to seal and brown. (If there are any livers with the birds, cook them too.) Lift them out and place in a large saucepan.

Fry the cubes of steak in the frying pan until sealed and starting to brown. Lift them out with a slotted spoon and place in the saucepan. Fry the onions in the frying pan for 5 minutes or until lightly browned. Add the mushrooms and fry for a further 2 minutes. Lift them out with a slotted spoon and place in the saucepan, leaving any fat and meat juices in the frying pan.

Stir the wine into the frying pan and cook gently, stirring constantly until all the meat juices are blended with the wine. Pour over the meats in the saucepan, scraping out the frying pan cleanly. Add the bayleaf (if used), redcurrant jelly, thyme, salt and freshly ground pepper. Crumble the Oxo cube in the hot water, stir and add to the saucepan. Cover with a lid or foil and bring to the boil. Reduce the heat and simmer very gently for 2-2½ hours or until the pigeons are very tender. Remove the pan from the heat, remove the bayleaf and allow to cool.

To make the pastry: Put the flour, suet and salt in a bowl. Add sufficient water to mix to a firm dough. Roll out the pastry on a lightly floured surface to a shape about 2 in. (5cm) larger all round than your pie dish. Cut a pastry lid to fit the dish, cut a strip from the remaining pastry and use to line the lip of the pie dish. Cut the remaining pastry into leaves and use to decorate the pie.

Heat the oven to 400°F (200°C) mark 6.

Place the pigeons in the pie dish and arrange the steak, onions and mushrooms around them. Pour over about half the gravy (keep the rest to serve separately with the pie). Dampen the lip of the dish and stick the pastry strip all around it. Brush with beaten egg, cover with the pastry lid and seal the edges. Brush with beaten egg, arrange the pastry leaves on top and brush with egg again.

Bake in the oven for 35 minutes or until crisp and golden brown. If the pie is not to be served immediately, cover it with foil and reduce the oven temperature to 325°F (160°C) mark 3. Heat the remaining gravy and serve with the pie.

Accompaniments: Serve with redcurrant jelly, creamy mashed potatoes and a green vegetable.

Serves 4.

Pigeon Pie.

COUNTRY GAME PIE

This is such a good idea for a buffet table or a very special large picnic. A variety of game can be used for the pie – whatever you can buy or any game that you might have in the freezer, though it is best to use younger birds because they are really tender. Use the smallest eggs you can buy as they look more decorative when the slices of pie are cut.

Filling

1 lb (450g) fat bacon or bacon pieces
1 small onion
1 young pheasant
1 roasting chicken (about 3 lb [1.3kg] in weight)
8 oz (225g) pork sausagemeat
1 level tsp grated nutmeg
1 rounded tbsp chopped parsley
2 level tsp salt
Plenty of freshly ground black pepper
10 small eggs, hard-boiled and shelled

Hot water crust pastry

1¼ lb (550g) plain flour
1 level tsp salt
8 oz (225g) lard
½ pt (300ml) water
1 egg, beaten (to glaze)

Jelly stock

½ oz (12½g) gelatine
1 tbsp sherry

Cooking time: About 2¾-3 hours.

Remove the rind and bone from the bacon. Mince the bacon with the onion and put in a large bowl. Remove the skin and bones from the birds and cut into small pieces. Add to the bowl with all the other filling ingredients except the eggs and mix thoroughly.

To make the pastry: Put the flour and salt in a bowl. Place the lard and water in a saucepan and heat until the lard has melted and the water is boiling. Pour immediately onto the flour and beat quickly with a wooden spoon until a smooth dough is formed. Allow to cool until hand-hot but not cold. Take two-thirds of the pastry and press out to line the base and sides of a 10 in. (25cm) loose-bottomed cake tin or pie mould.

Place half of the meat mixture in the pastry case. Make 10 dents in a circle around the meat mixture, put an egg in each and cover with the remaining meat mixture. Brush the edge of the pastry with a little beaten egg. Roll out the remaining pastry to a circle 10 in. (25cm) in diameter and cover the pie with it, sealing firmly. Trim off any surplus pastry, roll it out very thinly on a baking sheet and chill. Using a sharp knife, cut from the chilled pastry the letters 'Game Pie', of an appropriate size to fit on the top of the pie. Glaze the top with beaten egg, press on the 'game pie' pastry letters and glaze them. Make 4 holes in the pastry lid to allow the steam to escape.

Heat the oven to 425°F (220°C) mark 7.

Put all the bones from the birds in a heatproof casserole with ¾ pt (450ml) water, cover with a lid or foil and cook in the oven under the pie.

Place the cake tin or pie mould containing the game pie on a baking sheet and bake in the oven for 45 minutes-1 hour or until the pastry is browned. Reduce the oven temperature to 300°F (150°C) mark 2 and cook for a further 2 hours. Remove from the oven, leave the pie in the tin and allow to cool overnight.

The following day, strain the stock from the bones into a saucepan and boil rapidly until reduced to ½ pt (300ml). Season well with salt and pepper and allow to cool.

Put the gelatine in a small bowl with the sherry and 3 tbsp of stock and leave for 2-3 minutes to become sponge-like. Add the remaining stock, place the bowl in a saucepan of simmering water and heat until the stock is clear. Leave to cool but do not allow to set. Pour the jelly very carefully into the 4 holes made in the pastry lid. (It may be necessary to make the holes a little larger to pour in the stock.)

Leave the pie undisturbed in the tin. When it is quite cold, run a knife around the sides to free the pie. Turn it out, cut into wedges and serve.

Accompaniments: Serve with a variety of salads.

Serves 12.

Country Game Pie.

RABBIT CASSEROLE

This is a winter casserole which is very filling. If you can't get diced boneless rabbit, ask your butcher to cut a rabbit into small joints for you – allow about 1½ lb (675g) if on the bone – then increase the cooking time a little.

1 lb (450g) diced boned rabbit
1 oz (25g) plain flour
1 oz (25g) dripping or bacon fat
8 oz (225g) carrots, sliced
1 large onion, chopped
2 sticks of celery, sliced
¾ pt (450ml) water
1 chicken Oxo cube
Salt and pepper
1 bayleaf
Dumplings
4 oz (100g) self-raising flour
2 oz (50g) shredded suet
½ level tsp salt
1 level tbsp fresh, chopped parsley or mixed herbs
About 5-6 tbsp water

Cooking time: About 1½ hours.

Heat the oven to 350°F (180°C) mark 4.

Coat the diced rabbit in the flour. Melt the dripping in a frying pan and fry the rabbit quickly to seal for 3-4 minutes. Lift it out with a slotted spoon and place in a casserole. Add the vegetables to the pan and fry quickly for 2 minutes. Stir in any remaining flour and cook for 1 minute. Blend in the water and crumbled Oxo cube and bring to the boil, stirring constantly. Season well with salt and pepper and add the bayleaf. Pour into the casserole, cover with a lid or foil and cook in the oven for 1 hour. Taste and check seasoning. Remove the bayleaf.

To make the dumplings: Put the flour in a bowl with the suet, salt and herbs and mix to a soft but not sticky dough with the water. Form into 8 small balls and arrange on top of the casserole. Recover the casserole and return to the oven to cook for a further 30 minutes or until the

dumplings are well risen and the rabbit is tender.

Accompaniments: Unless your family is very hungry, potatoes are not really necessary with this casserole since it is so filling. Serve it with two vegetables such as braised celery and sprouts.

Serves 4.

RABBIT TERRINE

Boneless rabbit can be bought from some butchers and freezer centres, but you can carefully bone your own if you prefer. Chicken may be used instead, but usually it is more expensive.

4 oz (100g) streaky or fat pork
4 oz (100g) pig's liver
1 small onion
1 lb (450g) boned rabbit
½ level tsp dried thyme
3 level tbsp chopped parsley
Salt and pepper
Gherkin fans (to garnish)
Stuffed olives (to garnish)

Cooking time: About 1½ hours.

Heat the oven to 350°F (180°C) mark 4.

Remove the rind from the pork and cut into small pieces. Cut the liver into strips. Place the pork in a frying pan and fry gently for 5 minutes to allow the fat to run out, then add the liver and fry for a further 3 minutes. Coarsely mince the pork, liver, onion and rabbit into a bowl, add the thyme and parsley and season well with salt and pepper. Mix thoroughly and turn into a lightly greased 1 lb (450g) loaf tin, smooth the top of the mixture and cover with foil.

Stand the loaf tin in a roasting tin. Pour hot water into the roasting tin until the water comes halfway up the sides of the loaf tin. Cook in the oven for about 1½ hours. To test if the terrine is cooked, pierce the centre with a skewer: if

Top: Rabbit Casserole.
Bottom: Rabbit Terrine.

Rabbit Terrine continued from page 201.

clear juices run out, it is cooked. Remove from the oven and allow to cool, then chill overnight in the refrigerator. Turn out of the loaf tin and garnish with gherkin fans and stuffed olives. Serve whole or cut in slices, if preferred.

This dish can also be baked in a terrine or casserole as above, then cooled, chilled and garnished.

Accompaniments: This may be served with toast or brown bread as a starter, or as a main course with a variety of salads.

Serves 6.

OLD ENGLISH JUGGED HARE

Hare is very lean, fairly dry meat and therefore benefits from being soaked in a good marinade overnight. You can keep the blood from the hare and add it at the very end of the cooking time, but care should be taken not to allow it to boil after this, otherwise it will curdle and look horrid. As I am a bit of a coward and this so often happens, I leave out the blood.

1 jointed hare

Marinade
1 large onion, finely sliced
1 stick of celery, sliced
6 peppercorns
2 tbsp wine vinegar
2 tbsp oil
Large strips of peel from 1 lemon
¼ pt (150ml) inexpensive red wine

1 oz (25g) dripping
2 onions, chopped
2 sticks of celery, sliced
2 carrots, sliced
1 pt (600ml) water

1 red Oxo cube
2 tbsp redcurrant jelly
2 rounded tbsp cornflour
2 tbsp cold water
Salt and pepper

Cooking time: About 1½-2 hours.

Put the hare in a china or glass bowl. Blend together all the marinade ingredients and pour over the hare. Cover and leave in the refrigerator overnight.

The following day, lift out the hare and strain the marinade. Melt the dripping in a large saucepan, add the hare and fry quickly to brown. Drain off any spare dripping, add the vegetables, water, crumbled Oxo cube and the marinade and bring to the boil. Reduce the heat, cover with a lid or foil and simmer gently for 1½-2 hours or until the hare is tender (this will vary with the age of the hare).

Lift out the hare and place in a serving dish. Put the redcurrant jelly, cornflour and water in a small bowl and mix together. Stir into the saucepan and bring to the boil. Add plenty of salt and pepper and simmer for 2 minutes. Pour over the hare and serve.

Accompaniments: Forcemeat balls, creamed potatoes and red cabbage are delicious with this dish.

Serves 8.

Left: Old English Jugged Hare.
Right: Old English Game Pie *(recipe on page 204)*.

OLD ENGLISH GAME PIE

This is an excellent way of cooking older birds when you are not sure quite how old they are. If preferred, the meat can be taken off the bone just before putting it into the pie dish. Creaming butter with flour (beurre manié) is an ideal way of thickening casseroles and stews at the end of their cooking time.

2 tbsp oil
1 large, older pheasant
2 pigeons
1 large onion, sliced
1 large carrot, sliced
2 sticks of celery, sliced
½ bottle of inexpensive red wine
1 bayleaf
½ pt (300ml) water
Salt and pepper
2 oz (50g) butter
2 oz (50g) plain flour
2 tbsp redcurrant jelly
14 oz (397g) packet of puff pastry, thawed

Cooking time: About 2-3½ hours.

Heat the oil in a large saucepan and fry the pheasant and pigeons until golden brown all over. Drain off any excess fat, add the vegetables, wine, bayleaf and water and season with plenty of salt and pepper. Cover the pan with a lid or foil and simmer for 1½-3 hours, depending on how old you think the birds may be. Lift them out, cut into thin slices and arrange in a pie dish. Strain the stock into a small saucepan, remove the bayleaf and add the vegetables to the pie dish.

Cream the butter with the flour until a smooth paste is formed. Gradually add to the stock, whisking until smooth. When all the butter and flour mixture has been added, bring to the boil, then simmer until the gravy has thickened. Add the redcurrant jelly. Taste and check seasoning. Pour over the meat and allow to become quite cold.

Heat the oven to 425°F (220°C) mark 7.

Roll out the pastry on a lightly floured surface and cover the pie with it. Seal and crimp the edges, make a small slit in the centre to allow the steam to escape and use any pastry trimmings to decorate the top of the pie. Brush with a little milk and cook in the oven for 30-35 minutes or until the pastry is well risen and golden brown.

Accompaniments: Serve with creamed potatoes and Brussels sprouts.

Serves 6-8.

PHEASANT BONNE FEMME

Use large, older birds for this recipe. They have an excellent flavour if cooked carefully.

2 tbsp oil
1 oz (25g) butter
2 large, older pheasants
1 thick slice of streaky bacon, cut into strips (with rind removed)
1½ oz (40g) plain flour
¼ pt (150ml) inexpensive red wine
¾ pt (450ml) water
1 chicken Oxo cube
1 level tsp salt
Plenty of black pepper
16 button onions, peeled and left whole
6 oz (175g) button mushrooms
Sprigs of fresh parsley (to garnish)

Cooking time: About 2 hours.

Heat the oil and butter in a large shallow pan and brown the pheasants on all sides over moderate heat. Lift them out and place on a plate. Quickly fry the bacon in the fat remaining in the pan. Lift it out with a slotted spoon and place on the plate with the pheasants. Stir the flour into the pan and cook until pale golden brown. Gradually stir in the wine, water and crumbled Oxo cube and bring to the boil, stirring constantly until the sauce has thickened. Season with salt and freshly ground pepper. Return the pheasants and bacon to the pan, cover with a lid or foil and simmer gently for 1½ hours.

Add the onions and mushrooms and cook for a further 30 minutes or until the pheasants are tender (this will vary slightly with the age of the birds). Taste the sauce and check seasoning.

Lift out the pheasants and arrange on a warm serving dish. Either carve the pheasants into neat slices, or leave them whole and carve them at the table. Spoon over the sauce, garnish with sprigs of parsley and serve immediately.

Accompaniments: Serve with boiled potatoes and broccoli.

Serves 6.

CASSEROLE OF GUINEA FOWL

Guinea fowl are not always easy to obtain. They are now bred on farms, though they used to be wild game birds. They weigh up to about 3¾ lb (1.7kg), so try to buy a large one for this recipe.

12 oz (350g) chestnuts
3 tbsp oil
1 oz (25g) butter
1 large guinea fowl
2 oz (50g) plain flour
½ pt (300ml) inexpensive red wine
½ pt (300ml) water
1 chicken Oxo cube
8 oz (225g) onions, quartered
Thinly-peeled rind and juice of 1 orange
1 tsp redcurrant jelly
Salt
Black pepper

Cooking time: About 1½-2 hours.

Heat the oven to 325°F (160°C) mark 3.

Simmer the chestnuts in boiling water for about 20 minutes. Drain, remove the outer skin and return to the saucepan. Cover with fresh water and simmer for about 20 minutes, then drain well.

Heat 1 tbsp of oil in a frying pan with the butter and fry the guinea fowl until brown all over. Lift it out and place in a 4 pt (2.3l) heatproof casserole. Add the remaining oil to the pan with the chestnuts and fry quickly to brown. Lift them out with a slotted spoon and drain on kitchen paper.

Add the flour to the fat remaining in the pan and cook gently until browned. Stir in the wine, water and crumbled Oxo cube and bring to the boil, stirring constantly until the sauce has thickened. Pour over the guinea fowl.

Add the onions to the casserole with the orange rind, orange juice, redcurrant jelly, salt and freshly ground pepper. Cover with a lid or foil and cook in the oven for 1¼ hours.

Add the chestnuts, return to the oven and cook for a further 45 minutes or until the guinea fowl is tender. Taste and check seasoning. Remove the strips of orange rind.

Accompaniments: Serve with creamed potatoes and buttered broccoli.

Serves 4-6.

Photograph on following page.
Top: Casserole of Guinea Fowl.
Bottom: Pheasant Bonne Femme.

VEAL
RECIPES

Veal escalopes in breadcrumbs – a classic veal dish (see page 44 for cooking instructions). Serve with lemon slices and sprigs of fresh parsley.

BRAISED VEAL WITH MUSHROOM STUFFING

Veal tends to be expensive nowadays, but is always nice to serve for a special meal. By adding the stuffing, the meat goes further and looks good when carved.

3½ lb (1.6kg) shoulder of veal, boned
Salt and black pepper
4 sticks of celery, sliced
Butter
½ pt (300ml) dry cider

Mushroom stuffing

1 oz (25g) butter
1 onion, chopped
4 oz (100g) mushrooms, chopped
4 oz (100g) fresh white breadcrumbs
1 level tbsp chopped parsley
1 level tbsp chopped lemon thyme
Salt and pepper
1 egg, beaten

Sauce

2 level tbsp cornflour
½ pt (300ml) water
1 chicken Oxo cube

Cooking time: About 2¼ hours.

Heat the oven to 350°F (180°C) mark 4.

Place the veal flat and season well with salt and freshly ground pepper.

To make the stuffing: Melt the butter in a small saucepan, add the onion and fry gently for 5 minutes. Stir in the mushrooms and cook for a further 2-3 minutes. Remove from the heat, add the remaining stuffing ingredients and mix very well. Allow to cool. Spread the stuffing over the veal, roll up firmly and secure with string and, if necessary, 1 or 2 small skewers.

Place the veal and celery in a small roasting tin and spread over a little butter. Pour around the cider, loosely cover with foil and roast in the oven for about 2¼ hours. After the first hour remove the foil and baste well. When the joint is cooked, lift it out and place on a warm serving dish.

To make the sauce: Blend the cornflour with the water and crumbled Oxo cube, pour it into the roasting tin and bring to the boil, stirring until thickened. Simmer for 2 minutes. Taste and check seasoning. Strain the sauce into a gravy boat.

Accompaniments: While the oven is on, it is a good idea to cook a vegetable such as braised carrots that may be cooked under the joint, and serve sprinkled with plenty of chopped parsley. The joint is very good with jacket potatoes in winter, or with buttered new potatoes in summer.

Serves 8.

Braised Veal with Mushroom Stuffing.

OSSO BUCO

This rich Italian stew is traditionally made from knuckle of veal but, since knuckle is hard to find nowadays, you could use pie or shin veal instead.

1½ lb (675g) pie or shin veal
1 tbsp oil
½ oz (12½g) butter
3 carrots, sliced
2 sticks of celery, sliced
1 onion, chopped
1 clove of garlic, crushed
½ oz (12½g) plain flour
¼ pt (150ml) dry white wine
½ pt (300ml) water
1 chicken Oxo cube
14 oz (397g) can of peeled tomatoes
1 sprig of parsley
1 bayleaf
Salt and pepper

Cooking time: About 2½ hours.

Heat the oven to 325°F (160°C) mark 3.

Cut the meat into 1½ in. (3.5cm) pieces. Heat the oil in a frying pan, add the butter and fry the meat over moderate heat to brown. Lift it out with a slotted spoon and place in a 3 pt (1.7l) heatproof casserole. Add the vegetables to the fat remaining in the pan and fry lightly for 5 minutes. Stir in the flour and cook for 1 minute, then blend in the wine, water, crumbled Oxo cube and tomatoes and bring to the boil. Add the parsley, bayleaf, salt and pepper and pour the sauce over the veal. Cover the casserole and cook in the oven for about 2½ hours or until the veal is tender. Remove the sprig of parsley and bayleaf. Taste and check seasoning. Serve immediately.

Accompaniments: Serve with Duchesse potatoes and mixed vegetables.

Serves 4-6.

Top: Osso Buco.
Bottom: Blanquette de Veau.

BLANQUETTE DE VEAU

Sometimes stewing veal is difficult to obtain, although some butchers often sell pie veal which is very suitable for this dish. I have tried it with chicken too, which was equally successful.

1½ lb (675g) boned shoulder of veal or pie veal
2 onions
2 large carrots
3 bayleaves
1 tbsp lemon juice
Salt and pepper
6 oz (175g) button mushrooms
1½ oz (40g) butter
1½ oz (40g) plain flour
1 egg yolk
¼ pt (150ml) single cream

Cooking time: About 1½ hours.

Cut the veal into 1½ in. (3.5cm) pieces. Place in a saucepan, cover with cold water and bring to the boil. Strain the veal into a colander and rinse off the scum. Peel and quarter the onions and slice the carrots. Replace the veal pieces in the pan with the onions and carrots, add the bayleaves, lemon juice and plenty of salt and pepper. Cover with about 2 pt (1l) of water and bring to the boil. Cover with a lid and simmer for 1½ hours or until the veal is tender, adding the mushrooms 30 minutes before the end of the cooking time.

Melt the butter in a small saucepan, blend in the flour and cook over low heat for 1 minute. Lift out the veal and vegetables with a slotted spoon and arrange on a warm serving dish. Remove the bayleaves.

Boil the cooking liquor rapidly until reduced to 1 pt (600ml), then strain into the saucepan containing the butter and flour. Stir the sauce constantly until smooth, then bring to the boil and simmer for 3 minutes. Taste and check seasoning. Blend together the egg yolk and cream, remove the sauce from the heat and stir in the egg and cream mixture. Return to the heat to warm through but do not boil. Pour over the veal and serve.

Accompaniments: Serve with new or buttered potatoes and green beans.

Serves 4-6.

HURLINGHAM VEAL

Boned flank veal is a less expensive cut and needs to be roasted more slowly. Carve it in farly thick slices otherwise it will fall apart.

2½-3 lb (1.1-1.3kg) boned flank veal

Herb stuffing

6 oz (175g) streaky bacon, chopped

1 onion, chopped

4 oz (100g) fresh breadcrumbs

1 egg, beaten

1 tsp salt

Black pepper

Grated rind and juice of 1 lemon

3 sprigs of lemon thyme, chopped

2 tbsp chopped parsley

Thin gravy

1 chicken Oxo cube

3 tbsp sherry

½ pt (300ml) water

Garnish

Sprigs of fresh parsley

Lemon wedges

Cooking time: About 2 hours 20 minutes.

Heat the oven to 325°F (160°C) mark 3.

Remove any tough skin from the meat by slipping a very sharp knife just under the surface of the skin, then pulling it back by hand. Remove any excess fat. Place the meat flat on a board.

To make the stuffing: Heat the bacon in a saucepan without any fat. As the fat runs out, increase the heat. Add the onion and cook, stirring constantly until the bacon is slightly crisp and the onion is transparent. Add the remaining stuffing ingredients and mix well. Spread the stuffing over the meat, roll up firmly and secure with skewers.

Place the meat in a small roasting tin, cover loosely with foil and roast in the oven for 35 minutes to the lb (450g) plus an extra 35 minutes. Remove the foil after 1 hour to allow the meat to brown. Keep the foil on one side. Lift the meat from the tin, place on a heatproof plate, recover with the foil and return to the oven to keep warm. Drain the surplus fat from the tin, add the ½ pt (300ml) water, crumbled Oxo cube and sherry and bring to the boil. Taste and check seasoning. Garnish the veal with the parsley and lemon wedges and serve with the gravy.

Ideally, this dish should not be frozen. However, you can prepare it in advance by making the stuffing and using it to stuff the meat, but you should only freeze it for up to 3 weeks. Thaw it for 24 hours in the refrigerator before roasting as above.

Accompaniments: Serve with new potatoes and broccoli or green beans.

Serves 6-8.

Hurlingham Veal.

INDEX

RECIPES